AF531526

GOLF

DPH SPORTS SERIES

GOLF

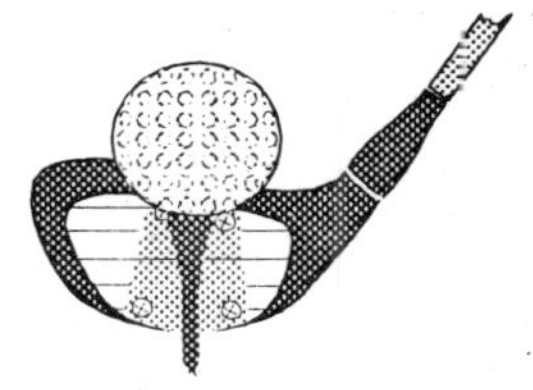

ASHOK KUMAR

DISCOVERY PUBLISHING HOUSE
New Delhi-110002

First Published-1999

Reprinted-2003

ISBN 81-7141-456-7

Published by:
DISCOVERY PUBLISHING HOUSE
4831/24, Ansari Road, Prahlad Street,
Daryaganj, New Delhi-110 002 *(INDIA)*
Phone: 3279245
Fax: 91-11-3253475

Tarun Offset Printers,

PREFACE

The need of having a sports series felt because today's situation of the world is not conducive to peace, all round there is destruction, despair, conflict and war; war if not between two nations then within the country itself. In a world where there are some 820 million people unemployed or under-employed, and where 86 million people are born every year, it is not surprising that one out of every four individuals lives in absolute poverty. The *Discovery Publishing House* by Publishing this series seeks to get positive response as—to means by which sports can promote and propagate peace and international cooperation. Sportsmen form a large identifiable cadre. We visualises a situation where a conscious efforts is made all over the world to train the sportspersons to spread the message of peace and international cooperation. Instead of peace keeping efforts through arms and army, the sportspersons may be used as soldiers of peace in a subtle manner. The effort is to make the realize the contribution of sports as a factor for sustainable development, peace keeping and international cooperation.

In developing countries, sports development cooperation is still in the need of justification and steadfast arguments. Many people ask the question "why invest in sports in developing countries for which water supply, health service and agriculture projects are much better suited? An apt reply to this question may be "for many of the people of a developing country, Sports is the only 'Sweaty' Leisure-time activity. Sports represents a moment of joy in the midst of hard poverty-stricken and dirty everyday life. Doing sports even makes one's work go more smoothly the next day.

This series will be useful to the sports promoters, organisers, coaches and other persons related or interested in sports.

Editor

CONTENTS

1

CONCEPTS OF GOLF

Understanding certain mechanical principles of clubhead action is important. Yet, many players ignore such information. Instead of directing their attention to the clubhead, they focus on what to do with some body part; head, shoulder, hip, knee, *ad infinitum*. If a ball is hit poorly, they may work on changing the movement of some body part, rather than examining the trouble source-club-face and ball contact. Simple concepts of *swing pattern, clubface and ball contact, and clubhead speed and distance* provide guideposts for swinging a golf club well and hitting good golf shots.

Questions on whether the swing is natural or unnatural are meaningless. People of all ages, even those with physical handicaps, have learned the golf swing but the problem is not in the movement. Attempting to execute the "how" by performing many details of action is one of the chief causes of learning difficulties. Trying to think of and perform many parts of the swing in two seconds is impossible and frustrating.

Emphasizing even one detail while swinging may cause trouble. No one questions that the left arm should remain fairly straight during a swing (putting excepted). However, when the cue "straight left arm" is carried beyond easy extension to an incorrect *stiff* position, the motion of swing is restricted. Over-emphasizing any detail can become an error that limits or distorts the whole swing.

Purpose is an important factor in determining the form of a motion. Suppose you wish to throw a ball straight up into the air. Your arm swings up sharply, and your weight shifts upward with the motion. This coordination occurs with-out thought. You neither think of swinging your arm up nor of shifting your weight upward. Rather, you think of throwing the ball straight up into the air and you do it!

Concentrating on the objective of the golf stroke-striking the ball to a target by swinging the club in a circular pattern-can develop a good swing. Novices fear that they cannot learn all the details of the swing. A player asks: "How can I remember to do all those things?" The encouraging answer, of course is that thinking of numerous details is unnecessary. Trust your body to supply and coordinate many particulars. The everyday motor you perform are evidence that this wonderful talent for coordination works almost automatically.

SWING PATTERN

A correct image of the golf swing is fundamental. To register the total concept of the arc, the full golf swing must be viewed from the front and the side. The swing is a circular motion on an inclined plane. While the clubhead gradually travels upward, it also travels around the body. The swing is three-dimensional. The swing to strike the ball a shorter distance varies from the full swing in length only. The distinguishing plane of the arc is less evident in the smaller swing made with shorter clubs. The clubhead follows a path of least resistance. The arc described by the clubhead may be a normal outcome of swinging the club to strike the ball from the ground to a distant target. Along with the total swing concept, correct images of how the clubhead should travel through the impact zone are important:

1. With relation to ground level, the clubhead travels close to the grass before and after ball contact.
2. With relation to the intended line of flight, the clubhead enters the contact area from inside the line of flight, travels on the line of flight, and on the follow-through, travels inside the intended line of ball flight. This is result of the clubhead travelling in an arc around you.

CLUBFACE AND BALL CONTACT

The flight and directional path of the ball can be directly related only to the contact of the clubface with the ball. Other factors may affect this contact, but in themselves, they do not propel the ball-only the clubface can do that.

When a ball is hit properly, the slant (loft) of the clubface determines the ball's upward flight. A struggling golfer may say: "I can't get the ball up," or "I can't get under the ball." Until this player stops trying to hit the ball up into the air, his or her troubles will continue and probably increase. Do not try to propel the ball upward.

The factors that determine the direction the ball will travel are the clubhead path through impact and the clubface position with relation to the clubhead path. *If* at ball contact the clubhead is travelling on the intended line of flight and if the clubface is at right angles to that line, the ball will travel straight along the intended path to the target. Golf requires a high degrees of accuracy. A small error in clubface and ball contact may cause a great error in shot result. Considering the size of the golf ball and the small hitting surface of the clubface, it is a wonder that so many fine golf shots are made.

CLUBHEAD SPEED AND DISTANCE

One distinguishing characteristic of a fine golf swing is the smooth, flowing acceleration of the clubhead. Many players neglect to drill on this quality of the swing, but not the expert golfers. The experts "tune" their swings to smoothness, ease, tempo, and rhythm. Their objective is to develop one swing that they can trust to repeat *and repeat*. This one smooth, accelerating swing produces great speed and distance-sometimes, a greater distance than the player expected. This is a surprising and pleasant happening, especially when a long tee shot is desired. But it is a "happening," and wise players know this. Their practice has paid off and will continue to do so. They are on the right track.

Experimentation is the downfall of many players in their quest for long-distance shots. They simply never get down to working on one swing and trusting that swing. Their swings are in a continual state of flux. These players would do well to follow the practices of fine golfers: to have the patience to clubhead speed, and the thus distance, to develop.

A typical mistake many players make is trying to swing faster or "harder" with certain clubs. For instance, after practice in hitting 7-iron shots, a player changes to hitting 5-iron shots. Knowing that the ball should travel about 20 yards farther, a player may instinctively try to "add something" to the swing to get more distance. This is a mistake. The longer club, with less clubface loft, will produce the added distance.

LEARNING BY LIMITATION

Imitation can be an aid or a hindrance to learning. Young people imitate easily and to a high degree. Unlike some adults, they do not imitate on the intellectual or analytical level, but rather on a "subconscious" level.

They grasp the *movement as a whole*. Pictures and feelings are registered, but not in words. Many caddies and young people have imitated fine golf swings, and this has played a part in their becoming good golfers. But when players try to copy minor swing details, swing styles, mannerisms, or idiosyncracies, they usually end up with what they copied-worthless details, not a better golf stroke.

In your imaginative brain centre, you probably have a picture of a golf swing, accompanied by a feeling for the stroke. This may be a copy of one swing or an impression that has evolved from seeing many golf swings. If the picture is of a whole swing in good from, and the feeling is one of ease and good timing, then this mental image can be an aid in swinging the golf club well.

PROGRESSION IN LEARNING THE SWINGS

Skillful golfers prepare to play a round of golf by starting their practice with the medium or short irons. They hit shots requiring less than the full swing and then work to the longer swings and the longer clubs. This makes sense. The short swing is an important stroke of the game. The feel and touch for all golf swings are best found and recovered in these short strokes. Short swings also serve as easy muscle and joint warm-ups for the full swing. The foregoing statements suggest that, if it is best to start learning golf with a particular swing, then the choice should be the small swing. The beginner need not delay working on the longer swings, but patience is recommended. You will achieve more success in striking the ball with the less complex short practice more enjoyable, as well as more effective. The putting stroke can be learned and practised right along with the other strokes.

THE REAL SECRET TO LEARNING GOLF

Useful guides can be given for learning golf and executing the swings, but no exact formula can be proposed. Who can confidently say that he or she has all the answers to learning golf or to hitting fine golf shots consistently? Novices watch champions, note a detail of the swing, and think they have "discovered the secret" of good golf. Of one thing you can be sure-the champion does not want to know this *secret*. The champion already knows the real secret: following the fundamental of good form in the grip, stance, and swing, and hitting thousands of golf balls in practice and play.

You will become proficient in swinging a golf club as you have become proficient in other motor skills-through repetition. Through trail and error, and through trail and success, you will discard unsuccessful swing actions and record successful swings in your "muscle memory" and in your subconscious. You can develop an effective golf swing only by following the basics of good form and by swinging a golf club many times.

2

GOLF GAME PRACTICE

SIX RULES FOR PRACTICE

Many golfers spend hours on the practice ground and achieve very little. Others spend a comparatively short period of time but produce the absolute maximum from a comparatively short session. The important point is always to make practice beneficial and constructive by sticking to a few basic rules. Here are six basic rules for helping you to extract the maximum possible benefit from your practice.

1. If you are at the stage of learning the game and are still a comparatively new golfer, make sure that you practise from good, consistent lies to encourage repetition. This will help you to groove the swing. Many long-handicapped golfers give themselves too much variation in the lie, trying to hit shots from good lies and bad lies without any rhyme or reason. As a rule it is much easier to groove a swing if you sit the ball up fairly well. Obviously, there is a time and place to practise from tight lies and from bad lies but that needs a slight change in technique. One of the main problems for the club golfer is that he will tend to pick the club up too much with a steep backswing and chop down on the ball. If you sit the ball badly you are more likely to encourage this. If you sit it up reasonably well you give yourself a far

better chance of encouraging the right sort of movements.

2. Always start practise sessions with one of the short to medium irons-say a 7-iron-and then work up gradually to the woods. The general rule is irons first, woods second. Club golfers often say that they have certain problems with their driver or fairway woods but hit the iron shots well. What in fact happens is that errors show up far more with the longer clubs. The clubs with fairly little loft will catch the ball around its middle- the equator-and so put on lots of sidespin. The more lofted clubs naturally catch the ball below centre and produce far more backspin and less sidespin. Errors therefore show up with short ones. If you start by working at sorting out problems with the medium iron, this will pay off as you work towards the long clubs. It is also as a rule far easier to get the feeling of a good swing with the irons than the woods. The irons have heavier heads and the woods the lightest the driver being the lightest club in the set. You can usually produce better clubhead feel by starting with the irons and moving on to the woods. This also encourages good timing and is a logical progression through the set of clubs. To the professional golfer teaching you, the errors in the swing will usually be fairly apparent with a 5 or 6-iron and he will usually want to correct errors by working with these clubs first, knowing that this will then improve the longer clubs.

3. *Pace yourself.* Don't rush. Many golfers practise with far too many balls in their practice bag and just hit them one after another without any real object in

mind. If practising on a driving range or where you have plenty of balls to hit, break the balls into fairly small groups, thinking of achieving some specific task with a group of ten or twelve balls rather than banging them away fairly mindlessly. Concentrate on quality not quantity. You will usually find professional golfers taking time over their practise.

They may start a practice session by a gentle loosening-up, hitting the balls fairly quickly one after another. But from then on each shot tends to be approached deliberately, trying to simulate as near as possible shots they want on the course. The inexperienced golfers, including many young would-be professionals, tend to think that improvement will easily happen simply by hitting a large number of golf balls. Certainly this can act as a strengthening process but may achieve very little. It is often far better to practise with one tube of twenty balls, hitting those in a meaningful way towards the target, collecting them and starting all over again. This focuses the attention on hitting each shot well rather than being careless. This is particularly important for the good golfer. The good golfer is trying to eliminate bad shots. His good shots are already three and often don't need any improvement. The single-figure-handicapped golfer's success is going to depend firstly on cutting out the bad shots and secondly on improving those bad shots that do creep in. There is no a golf course. The good player needs to hit the balls relatively slowly, as determined as he would be on a course to get rid of unwanted shots.

4. *Always aim at a target.* Sometimes you will be faced

with a practice ground which doesn't have any built-in targets. Don't simply stand and hit balls down the field without any aim in mind. Always walk down the field and set up some target to aim it. In this case it best to set the target at a specific distance, moving it or moving yourself so that the target is as nearly as possible at the correct distance. The ideal way of practising is to set out a reasonably large target which you can realistically hit from time to time. Most golfers practise to a post or to a flag but virtually every shot you hit is then going to be a failure. At best the good golfer will only hole a full shot once or twice a year. It is very easy to practice to a flag and become demoralized at shots, possibly not realizing how close they land to the target. In this way you can gradually get a sense of failure when what you need is to boost your confidence.

An ideal target for the good player is an open umbrella, firmly stuck in the ground at the distance you aim to hit. At least you get the satisfaction of landing a ball in it from time to time and it also gives you some sort of perspective for distance so that you can gauge how many yards to the side the ball is landing. With a flag on its own, your judgment is often poor. Another way of setting up a suitable target is to put your practice-ball bag down at the correct distance, with a closed umbrella jammed in the ground say five yards to each side of this. The exact width of your target will need to vary according to the length of shots you are hitting. This would give a good target for a good player hitting medium irons and should then be expanded for the longer-handicapped player or for the good player hitting long irons of drives. In this way you can assess just how well you are doing and can begin to monitor the kind of direction you are producing. If you are setting two objects to the side of your target area I would suggest always having something else halfway between the two, such as the practice-ball bag, so that you get used to aiming at a particular spot rather than between two obstacles.

5. If an a mission of fault finding and working through a problem, think things out logically, looking at the flight of the ball and the impact, and from there sort out any likely errors in the swing and particularly in the set-up. Make notes of your findings because almost certainly the problem will recur later. The process of sorting out problems needs to be thought out systematically. Analyse the flight of the ball in terms of where it started and how it has curved in the air. If there is a problem with the contact be specific over what is happening. In this way you can be fairly certain of what is causing this at impact and can begin to work backwards to find the error in the swing.

   All too often people will make changes-both amateurs and unfortunately some professional in their teaching-not by concentrating too much on the look of the swing. It is all too easy for people to have a set idea of what a good golf swing should look like. They may have in mind Ben Hogan. Tom Watson or perhaps Jack Nicklaus. At the first sign of faults all they do is to try to spot difference between their idea of the perfect golf swing and your swing. He does this, you do that. All you do is to work at changes in the appearance of the swing which in fact have no bearing on the kind of shots you are likely to produce-and may well be counter-productive. So think logically. You should also if possible make one change at a time so that you can begin to see the benefits. If for example you think there may be an error in the ball position experiment with this systematically. Don't try to change the ball position and, for example, alter the grip or you won't know which, if either, is having the effect.

6. If consolidating the swing practising for what you hope to achieve on the golf course, adopt exactly the same routine as you would on a course. Don't simply stand and hit balls, looking up once and thrashing them down the fairway, if this isn't what you do in play. If you line up shots from behind on the course then do the same on the practice ground. If you look up twice on the course do the same while practising. In this way you are actually rehearsing what you hope to do. All too often players have one way of approaching shots on the driving range or practice ground and then do something completely different on the course. This is not just in the swing and the set-up but stems right from the way in which they walk up to each shot, grip the club, aim and so on.

There are many ways in which practice can not only be made far more interesting but can also be as productive as possible. Here are some ideas for planning each practice session for players of different standards and with different problems.

A GENERAL PRACTICE SESSION

If you are consolidating your swing when things are

going reasonably well, work up through the short irons to the fairway woods and driver. An example would be to work with a bag of sixty balls, preferably all reasonably good and worth-while hitting. First of all work with the 8-iron, 6-iron and 4-iron. Let's assume you hit these 120 yards, 140 yards and 160 yards. The first stage is to pace out 160 yards on the practice ground and to out your practice bag or preferably an open umbrella into the ground at that point. Then go back to a distance 120 yards from the umbrella and hit a batch of twenty 8-irons. Separate the balls out into this group of twenty. Then go back another 20 yards to hit twenty balls with your 6-iron and finally back another 20 yards to hit with your 4-iron. Take the shots relatively slowly, meaning each one to go well. Line up the shots from behind or from the side in exactly the same way as you would on the golf course. If you are a club golfer you are basically looking at improving your good shots. If you are good player your concern is far more to eliminate bad shots. On every shot try to make the swing feel balanced and hold the end of the swing until the ball is virtually landing. In a had shot, be as specific as with a good shot in trying to hold the finish. This will tell you if the balance is good and will give you feedback about what has gone wrong in the swing. You may, for example, see the ball pushing out to the right and find yourself with the leg action blocked and the hip simply facing out to the right. You may on a very bad shot find yourself off balance and the end of the swing should give you a good clue to what is happening.

If your twenty balls with a specific club haven't gone well or the last one or two don't produce what you want, then stick to your pattern and go on to the next shot. If in moving to the longer club you simply can't get the same feels as you did fro the shorter one, then by all means go back a stage and hit a couple of shots with the shorter one to try to relate the feeling of one to the other. Having hit those balls, pick them up, moving the umbrella another 40 yards, say, for your driver, giving yourself a target 180 yards away for the fairway wood and, say, 200 yards away for your driver. Hit twenty balls of each and again make each shot count. When you collect the balls you should have a good idea of the pattern of shots you are producing and will be able to check the kind of distances the ball is travelling. The good golfer should always practise with the best possible practice the shots are flying. If at the end of your session with the woods you have the practice ground to yourself, you can get in some short game practice by pitching the balls with your sand iron to the umbrella until they are all in a reasonably collectable group.

PRACTISING ALIGNMENT AND DIRECTION

For many golfers one of the main problems is lining up correctly. Often what happens in a practice session is that a player will hit a couple of balls down the practice ground by way of loosening up and the place where those first two balls land he will assume to be target. Often he is simply allowing for a draw or a slice without realizing this. For all golfers, and particularly those with an alignment problem, it is essential to practise to a target. Players who have difficulty in aiming will often find that the problem is worsened in some situations. They may get an awkward feeling of having to aim across a certain fairway or from a tee which isn't pointing in the right direction. For these players it is essential to practise to a variety of targets indifferent directions, making a point of lining up each shot correctly and checking this if necessary with a club placed along the feet. If alignment is your problem there is often little point in putting a club down along your feet and hitting balls with this club in position. It is far better to go through your routine of lining up to a target, then putting the club down along your feet, walking down behind this and checking whether the alignment is correct. On the course you can't have any aid with a club along your feet so there is comparatively little point in doing this on a practice ground. Set four different targets to aim at across the practice ground, perhaps your practice bag, a couple of umbrellas or whatever. Take balls one or two at a time and set yourself up to the targets in turn. Alternatively you may find it just as beneficial to keep aiming at one target but to spread the balls out into four piles about five yards apart. Take two or three balls from one pile, move over to the next and so on. This may give you sufficient change in direction is that you will often fail to get the clubface and the feet you are going across a set direction is that you will often fail to get the set direction. You may, for example, get the clubface on target but find it awkward to position the feet and shoulders square. If this is the case, always try to line up the shot from behind, choosing a spot in front of the ball in line with your point and always start your lining-up process by standing feet together at right angles to the direction from ball to spot. In this way you should gradually find that you are able to cope with any awkward angles.

Let's assume that a round of golf for a fairly good player will comprise something like fourteen drives (assuming you have four part threes), ten medium irons and by six fairway woods. In order to monitor your success rate it is worth taking the balls out in specific groups of these numbers. If practising your driving take out fourteen balls and either hit these in two batches of seven or in one batch of fourteen, monitoring your success rate and so your progress. Similarly break the iron shots down into groups of ten, perhaps ten with a 6-iron or ten with a 4-iron and so on. Moving on to the fairway woods you can then tackle these in batches of six, monitoring a specific success rate for each group. For the good player developing a game it is in idea to keep a record of the successes of each, group, knowing, for example, whether you can hit iron shots at a rate of around eight out of ten, drives at say eleven out of fourteen success rate, and so on with the fairway woods. In this way you can try to push up your success rate session after session with a specific idea of progress and with a feeling of achievement.

Varying the clubs

One of the problems for the fairly inexperienced club golfer is moving from one club to another on the golf course. Very often on a practice ground he will get into the swing of things with a certain club, finding a set pattern to the address position and gradually getting comfortable with the grip. After a few shots he probably gets himself into the right position and starts hitting the ball well. On the golf course he probably finds it very difficult to move from one club to another, part of the problem then being to get the correct set-up and to grip the club properly. For the long-handicapped player it is essential to re-grip the club properly for every shot, never simply pulling forward one ball after another with the hands remaining locked. He will also find plenty of benefit in varying the clubs, learning to take out one club and then another, quickly becoming comfortable with each. Part of his practice session should definitely be to use say five different clubs, hitting one shot with the first, one with the second and so on until he can move from club to club in a totally comfortable way.

Another exercise on much the same lines for the club golfer is to imagine playing a specific round of golf or perhaps a few holes of that round. Again this is training him to change from one club to another and to be able to take up each club afresh without a feeling of awkwardness. This should follow a general practice routine of loosening up and hitting a few balls. He should then imagine himself playing on a specific course, starting by hitting the ball with a driver, then perhaps with a fairway wood and with a third shot with his wedge. From there he should imagine moving on to the second hole with another driver and perhaps a 4-iron and so on. In this way he will also begin to feel any shots on that particular course which cause problems. Very often he will find that holes which cause problems in reality also cause problems on the practice ground. Again it is a good way for the club golfer to learn to feel comfortable with every club.

Adopting a definite routine

This is advice specifically for the very good golfer but has real benefits for the club player too. In order to hit the ball well it essential to adopt as definite a routine as possible. Most golfers have far too much variation between what they do on the practice ground, what they do in play and what they do under pressure. Often their approach to shots will slow down quite dramatically under pressure, becoming pedantic and trying too hard, often rushing the swing and bringing out the worst in their golf.

As far as possible each shot on the practice ground should be played in the same routine being used in a pressure situation. Instead of this a player will often hit balls on the practice ground in a fairly carefree way, pulling the ball towards him, looking up once and simply hitting it. On the course he probably does something quite different lining up the shot from behind, now looking up a couple of times and fidgeting or having some other mannerism before hitting the ball. In a tournament or when tired or under pressure he probably alters this again, looking up a third or fourth time, shuffling the feet and making other unwanted movements.

The good player needs a definite routine so that he can almost set a stop watch from the moment he looks at the from behind to the moment he strikes it. The more repetition he can get, the better his chance of success on the course. For the good player it is essential to practise for the real thing by hitting the balls comparatively slowly and lining up each thoroughly and systematically. Every shot should be approached as though it is the real thing. Here again the player needs relatively few golf balls, walking round behind each to line it up properly and sorting out for himself his exact routine in terms of waggling the club in preparation, looking up to the target and so on. His precise method of lining up, setting the feet and attacking the ball should be monitored fully. He should also finish the swing and watch the ball in a fairly routine way, gradually developing the repetition which is needed for good play.

Practising driving

Let's assume once again that a round of golf consists of fourteen drives (with four par threes). To practise driving really meaningfully you need to have a definite target area in mind with something to give you guidance as to whether or not your drives would land on a fairway. For the good player I would suggest having two targets 30 yards apart, and something bang in the middle to aim for. Two rolled up umbrellas stuck in the ground can, for example, give side targets with a practice-ball bag strategically placed in the middle to aim at. The ball should then be approached in a fairly slow, routine way, working systematically at trying to get all fourteen well away and down the middle. This begins as a rule to produce a little pressure and competitive spirit even when practising on your own. You can gradually get the feel for your own success rate and monitor the accuracy of your shots.

Driving a specific course

For the top-class important part of the game. Without good driving he is always off to a bad start and struggling. If he is driving well, the course is made comparatively straightforward. The good player will also often want to feel that he needs to draw the ball or fade the ball or protect one side of the fairway or the other. An excellent exercise for the good player imagining himself playing the first hole, driving the second hole and so on. Some holes will require a specific kind of feel, moving the ball slightly one way or the other. Frequently this can give the player a feeling for the real thing. Again it is much more meaningful than simply hitting one drive after the other without any set pattern or real thought in mind.

Producing a variety of shots

Many good golfers practise on the practice ground without really knowing what they are trying to achieve. Often they will practise hitting a ball perfectly straight when on the course they then prefer to hit the ball with a slight fade or perhaps a slight draw. On a practice ground they may indeed see shots with a long or medium iron as requiring a perfectly straight flight but may then get on the golf course and see everything with the ball moving slightly left to right or slightly the other way. Again they are not practising for what they want to do under pressure. In this case a good player needs to be able to feel he is building up good ball control, and should experiment with moving the ball slightly from left to right or slightly from right to left. It is a mistake to stand fro too long trying to produce one particular shot in case a bad pattern to the swing is encouraged. The good player, or anyone who is trying to learn to work the ball with slight sidespin, should vary his pattern of shots to include every now and then two or three moved from right to left. A good pattern for the aspiring player is to hit two fades, two draws and ten straight shots followed by two draws, two fades and ten straight shots etc. In this way the player has to produce the correct shot the first time but without doing so many in succession that a fault is worked into the swing.

As a rule the really good player is unlikely to try to hit every drive perfectly straight. He may indeed want to feel that 90 per cent of the shots are hit with a straight flight but there will certainly be odd occasions when he feels he wants to fade or draw the ball. In a situation with out-of-bounds down the left of the fairway, for example, the player who hooks the ball will often feel most uncomfortable. He feels as though he has to start the ball miles out to the right and is then almost encouraging the hook which is going to get him into trouble. In some situations he simply cannot aim way out to the right, perhaps because of a line of trees or some other problem down the right-hand side of the fairway. In this situation the player should practise with a clearly defined line or obstacle down the left of the practice ground which he imagines to be the out-of-bounds mark, and preferably with an obstacle down the right hand side. In this way he should feel that he can aim down the left side of the fairway, moving the ball in with slight cut spin to land safely on the fairway. It is often not very constructive simply to practise this without any real target or object down by the fairway. He may simply fade the ball but without any real feeling of where he is starting it the reason for fading it and the area he is trying to land in. If he sets two targets 30 yards apart, this can encourage him to produce the correct type of shot and simulate what is going to happen on the course. He may also find great benefit from standing as far over to the left side of the practice ground as possible and actually learning to work the ball away from the defined sides of the practice ground, perhaps a row of trees or whatever. Similarly the player who slices the ball may be very afraid of the right-hand side of the course and again is well advised to practise for this particular shot by giving himself some obstacle on the right which represents out-of bounds or a pond, either planning on starting the ball out over it and drawing it back in or learning to hit the ball with a perfectly straight flight without allowing for and so encouraging an even worse slice.

For the good player the way of controlling the ball off the clubface with a drive is usually dependent on the relationship between the speed of the body unwinding and the clubhead. The feeling of fading the ball is usually one of unwinding the body rather early and if anything keeping the hands and clubhead slightly delayed. Conversely the feeling of drawing the ball is often one of being slightly slow with the legs and body in the unwind and speeding up the clubhead. To draw the ball the feeling is often one of having to sit slightly longer on the right foot in the change of directions at the top of the backswing, making quite sure that the clubhead reaches impact fractionally earlier in relation to the legs and body. The good player definitely needs to monitor his driving ensuring that the ball really does start off in the direction he means and with just a touch of the correct pattern of sidespin.

Competitive practice

A good practice session should prepare the player for a round of golf and should also prepare him for a competitive situation. Those players who achieve most from their practice usually set themselves certain standards and certain tasks to achieve. Some players are able to motivate themselves very well; others, particularly youngsters, are often better in a head-to-head competitive situation. The following are therefore some ideas of competitive practices. The first two can either be done by the player on his own or competing with others and the second two competitively between players.

Driving between targets

This depends on setting two side targets, preferably about 30 yards apart, and trying to drive the ball between these two targets. The idea is simply to work at getting the most possible in succession between the two targets. The player on his own improvement. This is also a good competitive practice particularly for youngsters. The players are all told to set up a ball and to hit the first drive. Those who fail stand back. The same thing happens again until there is an ultimate winner. Frequently the players who believe their driving is good and who have practised driving for an hour or so beforehand will immediately fail once there is a competitive element. It is a good way of bringing how to the would-be tournament golfer that his or her method may not stand up to the pressure of play or competition.

Distance from a target

A good way of practising iron shots is to hit a batch of twenty balls to a target at a specific distance, giving yourself specific points for all balls within a certain distance. Give yourself, for example, four points for any within twenty paces. Again this gives you a way of monitoring your success rate, and also makes absolutely certain that each ball counts. This is often a good competition for youngsters, either where there are two or three, each having differently marked golf balls, or as a team game with two teams again each having different-coloured balls or playing to two targets. One of the advantages with youngsters doing team practices like this is that they have to learn to play the shots with other people watching and this adds a competitive edge.

Head to-head driving

Another way of developing a competitive spirit with driving and for simulating pressure is to set players in a head-to-head driving competition. This can be done in one of two ways. The best way is to set two side obstacles 30 yards apart; the players take it in turns to play a drive along this imaginary faraway. They get a point for a success. With the proviso that the ball carries at least a certain distance. The second way is to have a definite target to aim for, monitoring which of them hits the ball closer in the direction of the target. With a team practice one can set up a form of knockout competition, playing off in pairs down to semifinals and final with a head-to-head driving competition of, say, ten drives each. This again is a very good way of encouraging youngsters to think sensibly about each shot and once more puts on a bit of pressure in preparation for coping with the golf course. Some find this extremely difficult but it does bring home to them the shortcoming in their game. This can also be adapted into two teams, players taking it in turns to hit their drive in front of team members, scoring one point for a success with each player in the team hitting perhaps, six drives. Once more there is the added pressure of having to do this in front of team members.

Competitive iron shots

Although a driving competition is usually the most popular with youngsters, an iron competition to a target can be equally beneficial if well thought out. The ideal form of practising iron shots in a competitive situation is to put an open umbrella at a specific distance, say 150 yards, with two obstacles about 10 yards to either side of this, rather depending on the standard of the players.

Players are divided into two teams, let's say five per team. They take it in turns to hit shot at a time, say six each in all, scoring five points for any ball which lands in the umbrella (not necessarily staying there) and one point for any ball which lands between the two outside marks. Again this is giving some purpose to practice and making each shot count.

For more advanced players of perhaps junior international standard an adaptation of this is to give as a target a larger area of five open umbrellas all placed together in a circle. They would then have a fairly good chance of hitting this target. The outside obstacles are again set 10 yards to the side of this. This scoring system now is to take the players in their teams, one at a time, scoring once more five points for a ball which pitches in the umbrella but losing all the points which the rest of the team has already scored for any shot which lands outside the two outside obstacles. By the last round this can put the players under heavy pressure, particularly if their team members have been building up a winning score over the opposing team.

ATTITUDE AND CONCENTRATION

— Confidence, the necessary ingredient for playing good golf, cannot be fantasy; it must be something real, based on the experience of striking many successful golf shots. You, like thousands of other golfers, can develop and improve your skill in the game through practice and playing.

— Applying negative labels to yourself, such as "I can't putt," "I can't aim," and "I can't use my 3-wood," leads to poor play.

— Accept responsibility for your shots. What someone

else says or does should not affect your game adversely. Blaming anyone or any "bad break" for a poor shot makes little sense. Keeps control of your game; then you can improve it.

— Golf requires patience and perseverance. Do not be disheartened by one or a few poor shots. An errant or" dubbed" shot may be a blessing in disguise: A fine recovery stroke may stimulate you to play an excellent round. A void letting yourself get "down." Perhaps, some brilliant shots still lie ahead.

— Golf requires concentration, exclusive attention to the shot being played, with no extraneous and disquieting thoughts. An often-heard expression about a poor shot is, "I didn't take enough time to concentrate." The implication that taking more time will assure concentration is erroneous. Time may allow disturbing and fearful ideas to enter into the planning. Be orderly and concise, select your objective, visualize the shot, and proceed to play the ball.

— "Playing " an opponent can take your mind off your game. Let your worthy opponent be you. Figure your best possible score for each hole and then compete against it.

— Being too intent may take the joy out of golf and slow down your progress. Remember that a certain amount of relaxation is necessary to swing the club effectively. Golf is a game for pleasure. Enjoy it.

As long as you play golf, you will take golf lessons-either from a golf teacher or from yourself in the form of self-coaching. This is the experience of all golfers, even the most expert tournament professionals.

To profit most from lessons:

— Be physically ready to take a lesson. Do warm-up exercises and practice hitting some golf balls. Without this preparation part of your lesson will be warm-up time, instead of all lesson time.

— Work with your instructor. When you are taking lessons, avoid working on pet theories of your own. To do an effective job of teaching, your instructor must know what you are trying to do.

— When you are given a cue about your swing, do not expect a miracle with the next shot. The result of a shot or two is not absolute proof of the worth or worthlessness of instruction.

— When you try to change a swing per instruction, the change may feel drastic; yet little or no change may be visible to a teacher. At such times, trust the instructor's observation.

— Golf classes provide general instruction in the fundamental and some individual coaching. There is good reason for individual help because all swings do not develop the same. The coaching given one person may not be useful to another.

— Avoid feeling disappointed and that you are failing to receive your money's worth if your instructor implies or says that your swing looks fine and that what you need is practice and play, not more instruction in swing analysis.

SELF-COACHING

Intelligent self-coaching builds your golf game; poor self-coaching destroys it. Your future golf game may be influenced most by your own teaching.

— If you have a persistent problem, taking a lesson from a competent teacher instead of continuing to work alone may save much frustration and time.

— You can gather a mass of data on golf swing from reading taking lessons, watching expert golfers, and listening to other players. Be intelligent and discriminating in evaluating these ideas. Are the concepts sound, and do they apply to you? Accumulating information has a bad and a good side: You may "jam" your brain with too much data, or you may be enlightened by a new and different approach to the swing.

— When poor shots pop into your game, do not panic and instantly begin a corrective program. Hitting a golf ball well requires precision. Anyone can have a lapse. If your stroke has been fairly consistent, give it a chance to return; do not tear it apart. If one club is giving you trouble, put it away and forget it. Later, practice with the club for short periods. Think about what to do right—not "what did I do wrong?"

— Remember—the hands are the connecting link with the club. They direct and transmit power. A fine sense of control with the fingers and hands is necessary to stroke the ball well. Sense the hands directing and controlling clubhead action.

Theories abound for hitting golf shots and correcting swings. At practice ranges, you can get "free" lessons by asking almost any player for advice. The value of some pointers is questionable, however. While many golfers like to relate the secrets to their success, their advice often varies from day to day: A tip that seems a miraculous cure day is discarded the next.

FITNESS FOR GOLF

Many athletes participate in training programs to increase their skills and to avoid joint and muscle strain. Well -chosen exercises can help to attain these goals as well as contribute to everyday good health. But exercises should be chosen? Books, articles, audio and video cassettes, and television programs overwhelm us with calisthenic choices.

Serious thought was given to presenting a series of conditioning exercises for golfers in this text. But an exercise program should begin, not with exercise, but with the individual—a consideration of the person's needs, present capabilities, and physical habits—which makes including one series of exercises for all readers questionable. In addition, in the short space that can be allotted to this subject in a golf book, the ramifications of exercise—such as precautions, uses, and exact details of performance—cannot be adequately explored. The content of this book therefore, has been confined to *golf* and to suggestions about how to make the best use of the physical activity of the game.

Perhaps the simplest and best advice for golfers is this: if you now walk the course, *keep walking*. If at present you are not walking the course but are physically able to do so, *start walking*. Leg strength is essential in swinging a golf club effectively. Keep your leg muscles in good tone, and treat your body and feel to the pleasure of treading on soft, grassy turf for about three miles.

Players required by the course management to rent and use a motorized cart should arrange with their riding partners to alternately walk and ride every other hole. Those players choosing to use a motorized cart because carrying a full, heavy set of clubs is too much of a burden can try carrying a partial set in a lightweight bag. The benefits derived from walking may be a good trade for using fewer clubs. Besides, some players discover little, if any, change in their games if they use fewer clubs.

One prominent golfer refers to the game played by golfers able to walk the course, but who choose to ride in a motor vehicle, as "cart golf". It is easy to agree with this golf purist: Too many people are failing to play the traditional game of golf, and too many are failing to derive its potential physical benefits.

Another piece of advice is to know what your body is capable of doing and accept its limitations. Use your body effectively; do not abuse it. Avoid attempting to swing a club in a fashion unsuitable to you.

The old cliche, "Keep your head down," leads overzealous followers of advice into trouble. On a full swing, they attempt to keep their heads in the address position long after the ball has been struck. Besides destroying the swing through the ball, this attempted restriction can lead to a real pain in the neck.

A questionable swing cue for some players is to keep the left flat on the ground in the backswing of a full swing. Golfers with great flexibility may have no difficulty with his restriction. But for the less supple golfer, trying to coil the upper body while inhibiting the turn and natural "give" of the lower body and legs is useless and risky. A free swing is difficult. Strenuously working one part of the back against a resisting part may cause a healthy back to become sensitive and a sensitive one to become painful. (Most golfers allow the left heel to rise slightly from the ground in the backswing of a full swing).

Nothing is so tempting to golfers as the idea of lengthening their drivers. One cue for this universal wish is to shift your hips forward on the downswing to get your body into the shot. Recalling the verse of a song may serve as a warning against taking this cue too seriously: "The thigh bone's connected to the hip bone the hip bone's connected to the backbone, the backbone's....." With a "super-distance" vision in mind, some golfers violently thrust their hips forward. But an exaggerated hip movement that does not blend in with the whole swing is useless and may render a person unfit for golf.

Golf swings vary because people vary. We can all develop good form that suits our particular body build and condition. When golfers attempt to move or restrict movement in ways that tax the body's natural ability, nothing is gained and a good deal may be lost.

THREE ERRORS IN BALL CONTACT

Topping

A topped ball is hit above its centre, thus imparting topspin to the ball. The ball may travel in the air a short distance and then dive to the ground or it may just roll along the ground. Attempting to hit the ball up into the air or to get under the ball often results in a topped shot. With such incorrect ideas in mind, the player is apt to swing the clubhead sharply upward through the impact zone, thus contacting the ball above its centre. The strong, upward clubhead action causes the head and body to move up. The body weight may fail to shift properly to the left foot; in extreme cases, the weight may shift back to the right side, with the left heel coming off the ground.

Another common error causing a topped shot is changing the focus of attention from the execution of the stroke to its result. Instead of completing a good swing through the ball, the tense and anxious player looks up quickly to see, "What happened?"

The early upward motion of the head at ball contact has fostered the most widely used correction of golf swings: "Keep your head down." The problem with using only this cue is that the real error is not addressed. The ball is topped with the clubhead—not the cranium. To correct the error of topping, attention—not an one symptom. The following cues can be helpful in eliminating the error of topping:

— Select the correct purpose for the swing: to contact the ball squarely and hit it to the target. The clubface loft, not any swing effort, will loft the ball into the air.

— Focus on the complete swing. Be patient about seeing the shot result.

— Avoid flinching through the impact area. The act of drawing away from the ball with the shoulders and arms pulls the clubhead up. Keep the shoulders and arms easy.

— Swing the clubhead low through the impact area. If the ball is hit from a tee, sweep out the tee as the ball is struck; if from the grass, sweep the grass after striking the ball.

— In addressing the ball, instead of looking at the top of the ball, watch a spot at the back of the ball where contact should be made.

— Think: "Hit the ball so it will travel low." With this thought in mind, the clubhead is likely to be swung close to the ground through impact.

STRIKING THE GROUND BEFORE BALL CONTACT-"FAT" SHOT

A "fat" shot occurs when, instead of swinging the hands, along with the clubhead, through the impact, area the player attempts to "flip" the clubhead at the ball. The clubhead is sent forward, while the hands and wrists almost come to a stop.

Shanking the ball

If shanking the ball were a common fault, the population of golfers might decrease considerably. shanking may be the most exasperating error in golf. This shot is hit with an iron, and the ball is contacted near the club, the rounded surface at the heel of the clubface. When the ball is struck with this rounded surface, the ball "squirts" out to the right. The word *shank* is taboo in golf conversation-golfers fear that the mere mention of the word will bring on the error! Opinions on corrections would fill a book but the following are possible solutions:

— Go back to the simple. Practice hitting short approach shots with a medium iron and work up to longer iron shots. Unless the swing is completely off, this may be the best correction, since it involves working on the positive and not fighting a fault.

— Avoid picking up the club on the backswing and applying extra effort can force the clubhead forward and outside of the intended ball flight line.

— Placing a tee in the ground just beyond the toe of

the clubhead and then swinging to avoid hitting the tee can help to correct the clubhead path.

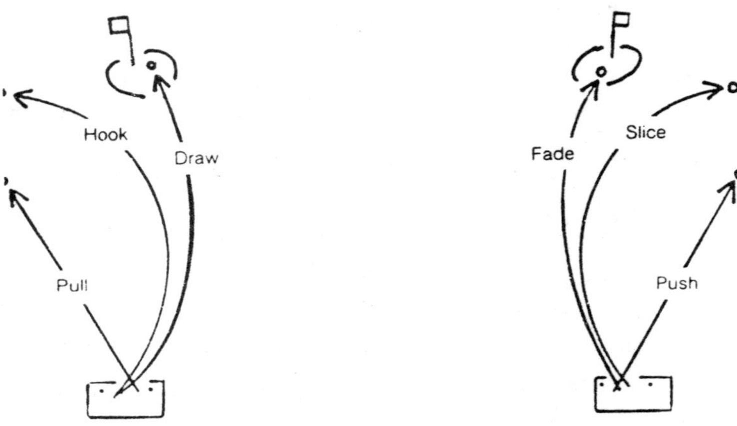

Fig 1: Director paths of golf shots

— Check the spot on the clubface where the ball us addressed. Addressing the ball out towards the toe of the clubface to allow for any error may be of temporary help.

DIRECTIONAL FLIGHT ERRORS

Why a golf shot travels off line to the right or left of the intended target should not be a mystery. To demonstrate how you can stroke a ball off line, try this experiment using a putter: Put a ball to a target about five feet away. Then, keeping the same stance and grip, putt a ball to the left of the target. If the ball rolled straight to the right or left, the putter face was at right angles to the clubhead path. If the ball rolled in a curved path with clockwise or counter clockwise spin, then the clubface was not perpendicular to the path of the club.

In baseball or softball, players hit balls to left, centre, and right fields by timing the swings so that the bat faces the target at impact. No change of stance is necessary. In tennis or table tennis, players hit shots to right, centre, or left courts; they even purposely put spin on the ball to deceive their opponents.

Whether the ports implement to strike a ball is a golf club, or racket the position of the striking surface and its path at ball contact determine the flight to the ball. This basic information is useful when examining errors in the directional flight of the golf ball.

Push and slice

Both push and slice shots travel to the right of the intended target. In a *push* shot, the path of the clubhead through the contact area is in a line toward the right of the target, and the clubface is perpendicular to this line. This produces a straight shot but off line to the right. In a *slice*, the path of the clubhead through contact can vary, but the clubface in relation to the path is open or facing to the right. This contact produces a horizontal, clockwise spin on the ball. As the spinning ball travels through the air, it curves to the right.

In considering the following corrections for these errors, assume that the grip and stance are correct and that the swing appears to be in good form.

— Being a fraction late in swinging the clubface to the square position at ball contact results in errant shots to the right. The ever-present urge to add effort at impact may cause the player to push the handle, leaving the clubface open. Also, a "quitting action" caused by anxiety and fear prevents the clubface from reaching the square position. Instead of confidently swinging the clubhead and maintaining the correct swing posture through impact, the player rises up, "comes off the ball" and leaves the clubface pointing to the right. Directing attention to swinging the clubface to the square position should help to correct these errors.

— If leaving the clubface open at impact has been persistent problem, it may feel as if the clubface is closed when it is finally swung to the square position. In some cases where the wrong feeling has been established, it is necessary to exaggerate—to try to swing the clubface to the closed position at ball contact. If, after such an attempt, the ball travels straight?

— When the ball first travels to the left and then curves to the right of the intended target, the clubhead path is from "outside-in". This action may be the result of trying to avoid a slice, trying to steer the ball away from the right. The cure may be taking many practice swings in the away from the right. Visualize the correct path through impact and swing on that line. Cut a swath of grass with the clubhead to check the path.

— Avoid trying to steer the ball straight or to get a straight follow-through. Trust that the swiftly swinging clubhead will travel in the correct path and strike the ball squarely.

— A poor correction is aiming to the left of the target. Such a practice fails to correct the error and usually compounds it.

An often-head correction for slicing is "hit inside-out." This may have some value for the person who has a very destroyed swing, with the clubhead travelling from far outside and cross the intended line of flight. Following only the cue "swing from inside-out", however, may increase the error of hitting to the right. The path of the clubhead through the contact area should be from inside the intended line-on the intended line—and then inside again.

A closed stance is suggested frequently to correct slicing. If the player takes a closed stance and has a feeling of aiming to the right, and then compensates for this aim by swinging the clubface over to direct the ball to the intended target, this stance would be an aid. But changing the stance does not necessarily change the direction of the shot. Trick-shot artists prove this: They can take any stance, stand on one foot, or even sit down and hit the ball in any direction they choose. The path of the clubhead through the impact area and the relation of the clubface to this path determines the directional flight of the ball.

Pull and hook

Both pull and hook shots travel to the left of the intended target. In the *pull* shot, the path of the clubhead through the contact area is on a line toward the left of the target, and the clubface is perpendicular to this line. This produces a straight shot but off line to the left.

In a *hook* shot, the path of the clubhead can vary, but the clubface in relation to the clubhead path is closed or facing to the left. This contact produces a horizontal, counter clockwise spin of the ball. As the spinning ball travels through the air, it curves to the left.

The errors of pulling and hooking are less common than pushing and slicing. Consider the following points to correct for the pull or hook:

— Check the grip, especially the right hand. If the club is held with the right palm facing skyward, an errant shot to the left is likely. During the swing, the right hand is apt to return to a more natural position thus closing the clubface.

— To change a habit of swinging the clubhead to a closed position at impact, it may be necessary to try to swing the clubhead through the ball with a feeling that the clubface is open. If the ball travels straight after such an effort, the clubface was square at ball contact.

— Trying to hit the ball an extra long distance and "slapping" at the ball often result in hooking the ball. When this error is corrected, the player may sense a dramatic change in the swing. It may feel as though the left hand and arm are in control of the downswing and follow-through and that the right hand is doing little or nothing to strike the ball.

— If you consistently pull the ball to the left of the target, check your stance and the ball position in relation to your feet. When a player pulls a ball. It may be obvious that he or she has turned the body too early in the impact zone. Fear of hitting to the right may cause a player to turn on the ball to direct it away from such a directional error.

At times, skilled players intentionally stroke a ball so that it curves in flight and ends up on target. The *draw* shot curves in flight from right to left, the *fade* shot from left to right. Changing the grip may affect the alignment of the clubface, thereby altering the directional ball flight.

PLAYING HINTS

— Be ready to play golf. Warm up before you play. Before stepping on the first tee, practice swinging the club, starting with the short swing. Do gentle stretching exercises and hold the stretch a few seconds. Avoid violent or "bouncing" exercises. Make easy movements that will relax the shoulder and neck area. As you play your round, stay easy so that you can use your muscles efficiently

— Learn the golf rules. Ignorance of the rules may you penalty strokes. Privileges extended by the rules may prove advantageous; for instance when you drop a ball back of a water hazard, you may choose a well-kept area of grass on which to drop the ball, provided that all the other provisions of the rules are followed.

— Play according to the rules and keep your score accurately. To do otherwise is deceiving yourself.

— Golf should be a congenial and friendly game. When all players are considerate of each other, the game is enjoyable. The golf course is not the place for a lot of talk idle chatter.

— If the course is in poor condition, improving the lie of the ball on the fairway (preferred lies or winter rules) may be condoned. Continued play of winter rules, however, is not golf. Accept the game's challenge-play the ball as it lies.

— Do not complain about the course. You choose the course; it does not choose you.

— No instruction on how to swing a club should be given during a round Swing cues given during play are seldom appreciated; usually, they are distracting to both coach and student.

— Assume that you are teeing off at a hole with an out of bounds along the right side of the fairway. Tee the ball toward the right side of the teeing ground and aim to shoot to the centre or slightly left of centre of the fairway. In similar circumstances, use this strategy of aiming away from trouble.

— In playing approach shots or putts from of the putting green, the flagstick may be attended, removed from the hole, or left in the hole. If the ball is played from off the putting green, there is no penalty if it strikes the unattended flagstick. When playing a shot from off the putting green, most players prefer to have the flagstick left in the hole and unattended. Sometimes, the stick acts as a backstop for a firmly hit or downhill shot. The ball may fall into the hole or end up inches away from the cup if and when it strikes the flagstick.

— Tee up the ball when playing an iron shot from the tee. It is easier to hit a ball from a tee than from the ground. To avoid possible interference by the tee when hitting with a high-lofted iron (the tee and the ball could be contacted simultaneously), loosen the turf (especially hard ground} around the tee as you place it in the turf, or use a broken tee. If the tee is struck, it can fly out of the ground easily, offering no resistance.

— Think of and play one shot at a time. Have a clear the purpose for each stroke. Avoid building up concern and tension about the next shot. For example, you see the ball roll into a distant bunker. The shot cannot be played from a distance-relax. When you reach the bunker, size up the situation, plan the shot, and play it.

— To select the correct club for a shot, consider: (1) the lie of the ball, (2) the desired distance, (3) special requirements for the situation, (4) course conditions and (5) your skill with the different clubs. If the choice is between two clubs in which you have equal confidence, generally play the longer club to the green. Being short of the green ("underclubbing") is a common fault.

— Learn different distances to the greens by spotting various objects, such as trees, bushes, and bunkers. Learn the "breaks" of the greens. Plan the most advantageous way to play each hole. Adjust your game to the course. If the ball is lying in a difficult position, on sparse grass, or on bare ground, take a practice swing over a spot similar in nature (if such a spot in near your ball). You have been faced the situation and will be less apt to be concerned about the lie.

— Play a safe shot if a daring one might put you in great trouble. If playing a safe shot costs an extra stroke to reach the putting green, a one-put green may make up for the stroke.

— Play your own game of golf. If your distance limit for a 7-iron is 120 yards, do not be challenged to hit 140 yards with a 7-iron simply because a member of your group can do so. Your objective is to score well, not to compete in a distance contest.

— Keep a record of your putts. In a corner of the scoring square for each hole, place a number indicating putts for the hole.

— Study your game after playing. If the game was fair or poor, what caused the trouble? Your swing? Carelessness? Lack of concentration? No warm-up? Too many putts? What are the solutions? If, however, you played a good or superb game, relax and enjoy the great feeling. You may even sit back and contemplate: "if a couple more of those putts had dropped....."

INSTRUCTIONS FOR THE NEW PLAYER

Your first experiences in playing golf can be especially pleasant if you are prepared to go on the course-that is, if you have acquired skill in the strokes and have a good general knowledge of the game.

You should be able to answer "yes" to the following questions.

— Are you able to sink many putts of two of three feet in length? On longer putts of 25 feet or more, can you hole out in two strokes 50 percent of the time?

— Have you developed some consistency in hitting shorter approach shots? Do you know which clubs to use for chip and pitch shots? Do you know how much to choke up on the club and how much swing to take for various distances, such as 20-40, and 60 yards?

— Have you developed some consistency in hitting the ball with the full swing? Do you know approximately how far you can hit the ball with each of the clubs in your set?

— Have you carefully studied and learned the safety precautions, the etiquette, and the golf rules? Are you willing to watch the conduct of the experienced golfer and to learn from your observations?

The following suggestions will help you:

— If available, play a course consisting of short holes. If your only choice is a full-length course, plan your game when the course is not crowed.

— In early games, most, if not all, players experience some anxious and tense times. To lesson and relieve these moments, playing every other hole allows time to relax, and just as important, time to learn by observing the play of others.

— If possible, have an experienced golfer guide you in correct conduct. But remember, no lengthy or detailed instruction should be asked for or given while playing on the course.

— You will most likely take more strokes than other players. You can help make up the time by walking rapidly between shots and by being alert to play in your group. Avoid delaying play.

— If necessary, be willing to modify your game to avoid delaying the play of others. For example, you have made several attempts to hit the ball from deep rough without success. Either pick up your ball and toss it in the fairway, or discontinue play on the hole and resume play at the next tee. You will be relieved of concern and tension; your playing companies and other golfers on the course will appreciate your thoughtfulness. Scores for early games are not so important that they merit delaying play.

— Golf is a complicated game. Be patient. With practice, study, and experience, you will soon be playing golf as it should be played.

PRACTICE

I knew a young professional once who devoured the doctrine that complete dedication brought success. He vowed to toil to his limits on the practice ground to achieve it. He had listened to the stirring stories of how Ben Hogan's hands bled through practice and how Henry Cotton worked until darkness and become to stooped that he was partially deformed for life. But they had become champions and, for him, it was clear proof that one only for out of the sport as much as one put into it. The truly successful had made efforts far in excess of their contemporaries and were rewarded accordingly.

The young professional began to work hard. He rose dawn so that the was ready to hit practice shots at first light. Every spare minute of his day was devoted to self-betterment and each night he full into bed totally exhausted but comforted by the satisfaction that he was giving everything to golf. There was no time in his life for distractions as he pursued this excellence. He never succeeded. Last head of, he was living in a commune of a Mediterranean holiday resort and earning a modest living by selling his painting to tourists. The clubs had gone and the dreams of greatness forgotten.

He was never quite sure where it all went wrong but this efforts went unrewarded so long that he lost heart. The truth was that he sealed his own failure with every hour he spent on the practice ground. He developed the biggest obstacle to successful golf......the practice ground mentality. In short, he had set himself such precise and narrow standards that he could think only in terms of the perfect shots. He had forgotten that the purpose of golf is an arithmetical count of strokes needed to guide the ball into the hole. Instead, the challenge of golf had become primarily the execution of the stoke, so that the ball was propelled on precise line and trajectory. That, after all, had been his only task as he toiled in solitude and out of context on the practice ground.

When he transferred that attitude to a golf course, and the specific demands of compiling a score over 18 holes, he was ill-equipped for the task. Whatever the first error, even though not seriously damaging, it was enough to put him into a despondent mood. More than this, there was no breath to his strategy nor flexibility to his thought and action. There was never been a perfect round of golf. But this young man embarked on it every time he teed up.

Thus had the art of hitting shots become more important than playing golf. He had sought a performance devoid of human error, and had completely misunderstood the purpose of practice.

There are three specific kinds of practice that must be followed for success. They are not optional, nor can they be taken out of sequence. Each form is directed at the various aspects that make a golfer efficient. No good score is ever made without them. The mistake of that young professional also was to assume he could dispense with these three forms of preparation, if ever realised they existed.

If he did it is doubtful whether he realised the difference and the specific roles each fulfils.......rather like teaching somebody the technique of acting—voice projection mannerisms and so forth—and then pitching him straight into the title role of King Lear without learning the words.

The theatrical analogy holds good because successful golf itself begins with the acquisition of good technique, a second that will repeat. It is the first form of practice by which the method is repeated until it becomes instinctive. The better player has less need to return to this drill with any frequency, though ordinary club golfers, with insufficient time to train their bodies, find themselves beset by problems of technique whenever they play and there fore constantly search for gimmicks, reminders or lessons to keep their under-used golf swing on a safe track. There is also the firm belief that constant repetition of the act at this stage induces, thereafter, a mild hypnotic state which is triggered at the moment of address and broken as soon as the swing is completed. Indeed, the best golfers are unaware of any conscious thought during the period of the swing when they are playing well and confess to a "cocooned" state of mind when at their best.

In its second form, practice is a kind of physical warm-up: a loosening of the muscles before the start of the round and more importantly an attempt to instill some essential sensitivity into the hands and fingers.

The third form of practice is extremely important and so subtle that it is often ignored or rather mistaken as part of the other two methods. Yet it is a distinct process and dress rehearsal for the real thing. It is the simulation of predicaments. On the practice ground there is little difference between the hitting ability of a great player like Jack Nicklaus and the rank and file golfers alongside him as they strike majestically into the far distance. When that requirement is transferred to a golf course, and a particularly tense situation. Nicklaus still produces that perfection while his lesser rivals falter. By a series of rituals, carefully planned and meticulously followed, it impossible to cultivate the state of mind which allows this natural golf to flow.

Before every championship, Jack Nicklaus roams the golf course and deliberately drops a golf ball into the worst positions he can find. He selects the toughest bunkers, nasty downhill lies without a blade of grass from which to play a delicate ship shot, heavy rough and semi-rough. I watched him follow this routine at Augusta before the US Masters and he explained: "I have now been everywhere on his course that shouldn't so there are no surprises." This thereby permitting him to play without inhibitions. His preparation also takes in extensive homework on the course to the extent of pacing its yardage from landmarks to aid his club selection.

This now has become a standard practice throughout world golf, although former US amateur champion Dean Beman is thought to have set the trend of authorities adopted a hard line and deemed the 200 yard marker post, common at one time at many course, as being against the rules.

Among his fellow professionals. Jack Nicklaus is regarded as the greatest extraordinary limits to suit his particular demands, the principle of preparedness holds true at every level. He, for example, will test the compression of every golf ball before deciding to use it. It is not possible in isolation to simulate the intensity of competition or the urgency of a short putt to in a match, but it is possible to prepare one's attitude. For example, the sole obligation in putting to get *one* golf ball into the hole without benefit of a second chance. That is as much a psychological as physical demand and some would argue that the act is almost a case of mind over matter. It follows that the only way to prepare (practice) is with one ball.

Players who stroke several golf balls towards the hole and claim they are perfecting their hitting action are diminishing their chances of success. They undermine the necessary mental strengthening by giving themselves a second chance. The entire will, and concentration, must be focussed on that single act. Nobody came closer to achieving that state in his practice than the South African Bobby Locke. Every practice stroke was a dress rehearsal for the real thing, and so his hitting rate was very slow compared to the machine-gun rapidity of fellow-practisers around him.

Locke had devised an inflexible routine. In his case preparation also included a kind of slow-motion approach to life on tournament days. Every act, even shaving and eating would be conducted with measured slowness to fix an unhurried tempo for his day. It required considerable planning to avoid the last-minute panics—a traffic jam or broken shoe lace—that might upset his equilibrium. But it worked and underlined the importance of adequate preparation for play.

The acquisition of a golf technique—practice in its basic form—can only be conducted under professional supervision because the expert eye spots faults and knows correct body positions. Unsupervised practice at this stage is dangerous primarily because it is possible to practice unknowingly a fault until it becomes a habit. The body itself can become very lazy and find a way to hit the ball without actually producing maximum efficiency.

Unless the muscles are stretched and the back turned away from the target and the downswing started in the proper manner, a player cannot achieve the appropriate kinetic energy to hit his weight and the ball will be struck well short of his limits. Therein lies a warning about all these substitute methods of preparation for enthusiasts who cannot spend time on the practice ground.

In fact, the great danger in moments of tension is to tighten up the grip and in so doing limit the backswing and produce error. The primary thought in the mind of every good player at that time is to hold the club as "lightly as possible". The correct grip pressure on a club should be akin to holding a small bird in firm but not vice-like fashion. The traditional argument is that the swing itself is the best muscle strengthening and conditioning for golf and no amount of sit-ups, squats and press-ups will supplant an action itself will build the required muscles. The counter claims are that this holds only if the proper swing is practised and that, anyway, latecomers to the game cannot hope to build muscles in this way.

However, there is exercise which serves a variety of purposes and does not require the golfer to hit hundreds of golf balls. It is ideal action for enthusiasts with not much time to spare. Devised Henry Cotton, it entails the simple action of hitting a car tyre laid flat on the ground and preferably against a wall. With short, sharp wrist-breaks, the clubhead is directed at the tyre tread rapidly in spurts of between 50 and 100 strikes. The tension in the forearms begins to build. The back muscles begin to bear some strain. So, too do the shoulders and upper arms. At first the hands will start to move anti-clockwise on the clubshaft through the force of rapid impact. This, says Cotton, is a sign of weakness that must be eradicated and only when the hands do not move from the original position after, say, 100 hits, are they of adequate strength.

With the Cotton method there is no danger that the strain imposed on arms and hands will minimize their sensitivity, for the simple reason that they are undergoing an inevitable grip-tightening that exists on impact in the swing. What also happens very quickly with this rapid wrist-hitting is an awareness that the right hand is delivering the blow involuntarily while the left hand brings it towards the target. If an occasional full backswing is then introduced into the sequence, the body itself will adopt the proper hitting position automatically as the clubhead makes impact with the tyre while the legs and lower trunk developing the necessary momentum. Four or five 100-hit sessions at home, even an hour or so before play, is sufficient to tone the muscles and more importantly develop the essential clubhead speed that determines power and direction. In its way, it is a kind of over-training that is a customary part of any athletic programme.

Some players wield a heavy iron bar, golf club style, to enliven the muscles. Even a garden rake or spade will do the trick. It is also possible to acquire a weighted club for that purpose or to attach a weight to a normal club. The trouble however, is that all of these devices lack the essential feel of impact that is part of the golf swing.

Many top players have their own ideas on how to prepare physically on the day of a match. They give themselves plenty of time to reach the course before they are due to tee off. Even after a practice session which starts with a few wedge shots to restore feeling to the hands and to rehearse the crucial part of the swing—impact itself-they work through the mid-irons, long-irons to the woods by which time the back muscles have loosened for these fuller strokes. Even then they are likely to try a few muscle looseness on the first tee, perhaps by swinging two club together or linking a club between the inner elbows across the back, staring at a spot on the ground, then pushing the left shoulder under the chin to adopt a top of backswing position. The body is then twisted so the right shoulder is under the chin. The exercise is repeated several times. This is ideal for sluggish bodies and ensure a full shoulder turn off the first tee.

All of this diligent effort will be wasted unless preparation is total and this means being also prepared for any eventuality. After ensuring that, it is time to play. You are as ready as you will ever be.

Required skills apart, the other reason for the game's enduring challenge is that the pitch itself never remains the same. Unlike tennis, soccer, football and cricket, which function within clear specifications and lead to a narrowing of precise skills—i.e. the tennis player learns to serve a ball to the correct spot be he at Wimbledon or Flushing Meadow—no such reliable limits exist in golf.

The golfer can find himself required to tackle a hard, featureless seashore where the ball has to be kept low to cheat the wind and played short to run over the hard ground to the green; or if he plays a lush parkland course, he must adjust his technique so that the ball is struck full and high with much backspin to stop abruptly on the soft green; while from sparse heathland fairways he must take the ball cleanly to prevent the clubhead jarring on the hard terrain.

Then again, each golf course completely changes character and mood with the weather; a parkland course becomes as fast as a seaside links through lack of rain with the additional problem that the hazards were planned for less fiery conditions and, by the same perverse token, a links becomes as docile as a dartboard when becalmed in constant rain.

This, then, is the other challenge of golf because if the basic task is to master the striking of a golf ball, its application over various stretches of countryside is the logical test of that accomplishment. The golf hole itself a test to be negotiated in whatever manner you choose using the scope the 14 clubs in your golf bag afford you. It means there is no "proper" way to play any hole except the method which secures the best score as American professional Paul Runyan demonstrated on Merion's last hole when he realised he should not hit his tee shot 200 yards over the trouble to reach the fairway. Instead he wedged to the forward tee, then hammered his four wood towards the green for a chip and putt and cleverly devised par four.

For short-hitting Runyan it was the only way to overcome a formidable obstacle but the real problem arises when the test itself is intrinsically unfair, either because it is ill-conceived or out-of-date. American architect Robert Trent Jones was asked to redesign a course that had been built in the days when a tee shot barely touched 220 yards, and discovered that at least 80 bunkers, all relevant to their time, were no longer threats to modern play.

If the basic purpose of a golf hole is to seek out the good player and reward his endeavours then it follows that diminishing skills must also be graded and even penalized by means of hazards, either sand, water, or what the old architects called "floral hazards"-trees, shrubs and bushes.

Essentially the sand trap not only punishes a bad shot but protects a green from such a stroke while, in the fairway, fulfils the secondary role of directing traffic-or rather indicating a prescribed route to the green which, if ignored causes additional problems for the subsequent shot. In fact where this does not happen, it is fairly safe to conclude the hole is not only weak but unfair and incapable of rewarding superior performance. Consider the first hole on the North Course of La Manga in Spain. The fairway doglegs to the left and a bunker has been set in the corner to oblige golfers to follow the defined route. The trouble is that even the correct drive strung between those two bunkers flanking the fairways holds no advantage because the green is guarded by a huge trap which stretches almost across the width of the fairway and so threatens approach shots from every angle.

There is, therefore, no proportionate reward because all play has been reduced to a crude level of caution. In fact, there is no proper way into the green that could persuade a player standing on the tee how the hole should be played. If the bunker had been cut back and balanced by another on the right side of the green, a clear entrance would exist. Thus the big-hitter who cuts the corner with his drive would negotiate the left hand bunker at the green, admittedly with a short range and more accurate club, while the orthodox hitter faces the open road with a longer club thereby providing the classic confrontation between tactics and skills.

However, opinions are still divided on whether there should be an accepted alternative strategy to the playing of such short holes. While Charles Hutchinson wrote in 1904, "a short hole should be bristling with hazards to demand the perfect tee shot to be played", he could have had no idea how bunker play itself would be raised to an art from by top players, indignant if their recovery shots finish more than 12 inches from the flag.

To combat this widening expertise, the modern trend is to protect a green with water because there is a finality about the error of a bad shot sinking to the watery depths that no golf skill can redeem. But even this practice can reach daft extremes as the short 17th on the Tournament Players Club in Jacksonville, Florida, demonstrates. The entire green stands in a lake and is connected to the mainland by a narrow path. It is the terror of all who play there because there is no graded penalty even for the tee shot that misses the green by a fraction of an inch.

In truth, short holes do not need to be such all-or-nothing perils, as anyone who has ever tried to make par on the 126-yard Postage Stamp at Royal Troon on a windy day will testify, particularly the German amateur Herman Tissies, who in the 1950 British Open took 15 strokes there after hitting recoveries with expensive monotony from one bunker to another.

What makes the Postage Stamp-unwittingly christened in 1923 by the Scottish champion and designer Willie Park, who said the small green had a "pitching surface skimmed down to the size of a postage stamp-is simply the angle at which it has to be played in the prevailing wind which gusts round the hill that stands to the left of the green.

The basic principles of any golf course layout, for which a minimum 120 acres are required, is that it pays heed to terrain, the prevailing wind and other directional factors, so that such other irritations as playing the last hole into a blinding sunset are avoided. In the past, architects tried to set the holes in a series of triangles to test a player's ability in the wind from all quarters. The ideal layout, however, has two loops of nine holes which start and finish at the clubhouse and preferably contain par fives (over 475 yards) that are balanced by par threes (up to 250 yards) in both outward and inward halves.

The terms "outward" and "inward" derive from the Old Course at St Andrews, where the holes run out along the shore, then follow a homeward path back. The major criticism that can be levelled at the Old Course is that it favours one kind of golf stroke-the hook taking the ball left-because it is the safest trajectory on this narrow strip, with out-of bounds to the right-hand side on both outward and inward holes.

Generally, a bunker is placed around 200 yards from the two to catch the sliced shot on the right-hand side of the fairway while the hazard for the hook, always a more powerful shot, is located 20-30 yards farther on. Theoretically, therefore, the left-hander should have no problems because, with his mirror image swing, both types of bad shots should avoid the right-handed hazards.

In one important respect, the golf course has much in common with the bowling green and cricket pitch in that the texture of the turf is critical to the standard of play.

The green requires a fine, but not necessarily thick, growth to produce a surface as true as a billiard table. Obviously the tee must be more hard-wearing, particularly on short holes where divots are taken (although the trick here is to have a teeing ground large enough for the markers to be moved round frequently, so the ground can recover) and like the fairways need a tough addition to the grass mixture. The danger on the fairways is that too much attention, through excessive watering and fertilising, encourages an invasion of rye-grass. While this can look superbly green and lush, it can be quite detrimental making clean contact for maximum spin on the ball. It is the cause of the notorious "flyer" when the ball is hit from long grass and travels distance much greater than expected from the club.

In hotter climes, it is essential to provide extensive cover for the ground, which is why varieties of grass that spread quickly across the surface and produce a dense turf are used. This can lead, however, to a "nap" on the greens: the tiny grass stalks tend to lie in a particular direction and affect the movement of the ball, slowing it against the "gram" and quickening it when with it also creates problems of aim and touch when the putt travels across the "grain".

That said, the character of a good green, its receptive powers and its speed, depended on proper construction. While there are accepted variations, the basic pattern calls for a solid base of gravel or stones, through which drainage pipes are laid, to be covered with a layer of sand and then about nine inches of top soil. Most greenkeepers and designers prefer to seed greens rather than laying down turf so that the grass develops its own inherent and durable strength. In some parts of the United States the all-sand green—just a nine-inch layer on top of gravel and the drainage system, works admirably. No top soil is required, and the drainage is remarkably swift but the balance of nutrients to assist the growth of the grass is so critical that it still in the experimental stages in Europe.

The design of any green makes provision for a variety of pin placements, selected with wind conditions and bunker positions in mind. Hugh Wilson, the great American architect, was so painstaking about the precise location of his bunkers that he laid out white sheets on the fairways and around the greens to determine whether the overall effect pleased the eye, suited the landscape and influenced play. Only then, did he start digging. The practice worked so well at Merion, one of the shortest championship courses in the world, that during the 1971 American Open nobody beat par for 72 holes, despite the improvements in golf technique and equipment.

The pursuit of golf on more than 20,000 golf courses in all parts of the world has tested man's ingenuity and skill not only to produce grass that will thrive in all conditions but to find a way of making greens, even where grass will not grow. In certain African and Middle Eastern states, the answer is a "brown"-a compacted mixture of oil and sand that is rolled frequently to provide a reasonable putting surface for players who, anyway, carry their own piece of plastic turf from which they play all other shots.

Golf at its highest point is played at Tuctu in which rarified atmosphere even moderate hitters look impressive because the ball flies farther. In truth, any scrap of land will suit the purpose of golf and fairways are to be found on terrain that also serves as Swiss ski slopes, aimed the tombs of a burial ground in Delhi and even running through a discussed missile base in Norfolk. Golf courses can be built on undisguised pastures on high-priced real estate. They all offer the common challenge to skill—even the bad ones.

3

FLIGHT OF THE BALL

The 'set-up', which includes posture, is another part of golf that is very easy to achieve; yet only a few players take the trouble to follow the basic rules. These simple rules are, stand tall, with the back straight, the legs slightly bent and the feet square to the target, about shoulder width apart. One normally finds that a player who walks with a long, loping stride, will adopt a wide stance when playing golf. Of course, the reverse is also the case. A person who takes small steps usually plays golf with a narrow stance. The reason for this is that they have found their own point of balance in walking, and use the same point of balance for any other activity. Variations are permissible in golf, like anything else, but only slight deviations from the basics are sensible for consistency. After taking hold of the club and adopting this tall posture, with the back fairly straight, and the head high, gently lower the club to the ball—flexing the knees, and bending the back forward, so the club rests on the grass behind the ball.

We always recommend that the feet, hips and shoulders should be in line with—or square to—the target, fairway or flag, depending on which shot is being played. This applies to nearly every long shot in golf. Many good players allow their left foot to open or point outwards at the address position. This does, however, restrict the backswing and is only recommended for supple players. Allowing the left foot to point outwards does assist the body to turn through the left foot to point outwards does assist the body to turn through.

Study the top and bottom edges of your clubs. Many people close the clubface because they aim the top edge of their iron clubs. If you look you will see that the edges of the clubhead are at different angles. The correct edge to aim at the target is the bottom of the club. If the top edge is aimed, the ball will almost certainly fly to the left. The reason for this, is that it is the leading (or bottom) edge which strikes the ball first, and obviously affects the ball immediately on contact. So always aim the clubface carefully with the bottom edge aimed squarely at the target and flat on the ground. Watch a good pro prepare for each shot and copy him.

Care, too, must be given to the actual position of the ball at address. For wooden club shots, particularly with the driver, the ball should be positioned opposite the inside of the left foot. This position hardly varies with good players, so it is worth getting right at the very start. For the middle irons, position the ball midway between the feet; and for the shorter irons, slightly back of centre.

In finding these important address positions, be extremely careful to keep the hips and shoulders square to the target line. It is easy to allow the head and shoulders to aim to the left, so get the feeling of staying behind the ball. We mention the head moving forward, as nearly all great players make a conscious effort to move the head slightly to the right of the ball. The great Jack Nicklaus is a perfect example of this. He makes a deliberate effort to move his chin towards his right shoulder, before starting his backswing. This helps his swing to follow the correct path on the backswing and downswing. Once this address position has been found, check the hand and ball positions. If a line is taken from the clubhead, on up the shaft, the hands should be about level with the navel.

We have heard good players recommend that the hands should be set ahead of the ball, but this changes the position of the clubhead behind it, and can cause other complications which we will discuss at a later stage. Quite simply, aim the clubhead at the target, and the shaft at your navel. This will ensure the correct aim and positioning. Just follow Sandy Lyle's advice: 'You can slave away for as long as you like on the practice ground, bashing balls, but it all boils down in the end to realizing that the set-up makes or ruins nearly every shot you are likely to hit.' This is indeed good advice from one of our best players who does, himself, have trouble at times with his set-up. In fact, whenever good players have trouble with their game they seek advice from friends and fellow competitors, and the most consistent error usually is found in their set-up. The golf swing only changes when the aim changes.

Whilst setting-up, it is better to keep the overall weight on the heels of the feet rather than on the toes. This helps the body turn rather than topple over as one would if the weight were on the toes. It also keeps golf club on the inside path on the backswing which we all know is the correct swing line. The Greatest Problem with golfers today (and indeed with teaching the game) is that two important factors are not fully understood.

We'll attack this second problem in two parts. First, we'll explain the mechanics of the club and the ball—what happens at impact that make the ball behave the way it does. Second, we'll give you the means whereby you can analyse the flight of the ball and determine how to correct undesirable flights (hooks, slices, too high, too low, and so on).

THE STRAIGHT BALL—AND OTHERS

A golf ball flies in a certain pattern not by chance but because of two factors: the path of the swing through impact and the direction in which the clubface is aimed at impact. For a ball to fly straight, the path of the swing through impact must be as we have taught you, from inside the target line before impact to square at impact to inside the target line after impact, and the clubface must be square to the target line at impact. Any other swing path or clubface alignment will result in something other than a straight shot to the target.

If a ball is pulled (flies straight to the left), the path of the swing was more from outside the target line before impact to inside the target line after impact than the correct inside-to-square-to-inside swing path. And the reason the ball flew straight to the left rather than curving is that the clubface was exactly square to this faulty swing path at impact. If a ball is pushed (flies straight to the right), the opposite applies: The path of the swing was too much from the inside toward the outside and, again, the clubface was exactly square to this faulty swing path at impact.

A slice (curve to the right) or a hook (curve to the

left) occurs because the clubface at impact is respectively open or closed in relation to the swing path. If the clubface is open, the clubface imparts clockwise spin to the ball (looking from a position directly above the ball at impact) and the ball curves to the right. If the clubface is closed, counter-clockwise spin has been imparted to the ball, curving it to the left. In the case of either the slice or the hook, there can be only three basic variations.

Slice

1. The ball starts to the left of the target line, then curves to the right.
2. The ball starts straight, then curves to the right.
3. The ball starts to the right of the target line and curves farther to the right.

Hook

1. The ball starts to the right of the target line, then curves to the left.
2. The ball starts straight, then curves to the left.
3. The ball starts to the left of the target line and curves farther to the left.

CORRECTING THE CURVE BALLS

The correct a sliced or a hooked flight, you have to straighten out the curve first, then correct any deviation to the left or right of target. If, for example, your ball is starting to the right and slicing farther to the right, you must first get rid of the slice so that you are hitting straight to the right. After that it becomes a comparatively simple matter to correct the swing so that the ball flies straight to the target. If your initial move is to try to compensate for the ball finishing to the right or left of target—and this is typically what the average golfer attempts to do—you merely compound the problem. Let's suppose the ball starts a little to the right of the target line and then, at the end of its flight, slices to the right and finishes in the right rough. The golfer sees where the ball has finished and his first move is to try to make the ball fly more to the left. So he alters his setup so that his body is aligned to the left of target and, for good measure, he tries to pull the ball to the left. His state is now worse than it was.

The path of the swing will now be more to the left, but the clubface will be more open in relation to that swing path. The result will be a shot that starts to the left of target but slices to the right more viciously than before.

Bearing this procedure in mind, let's consider the specific faulty flights of the ball.

Slice (Type 1). Ball starts to the left of the target line, then curves to the right.

This is the most common type of slice-a real "slicer's slice," if you like. Since the ball starts left, the swing path through impact is obviously from outside to in, and the clubface position at impact is open to the swing path.

The first thing to correct is the open clubface position at impact that causes the curve to the right. To do this, you should:

1. Check clubface is not set open to the swing path in the setup. (This by itself could cause the slice.)

2. Check your hold is not what is actinically called too "weak," which means that either the left hand or both hands are turned too far to the left. Even if the club were set square to the swing path, a "weak" hold would result in the clubface opening at impact.
3. Check you are not opening the clubface during the swing. Use the "swing-and-stop" method to make certain you have not rolled the clubface open going back. Also check for a free arm swing through the ball; trying to "push" the arms through can leave the clubface in an open position at impact.

If you have taken steps 1, 2, and 3, and you still get a curve to the right, you will have to consider turning both hands slightly to the right into what is called a "strong" position. The hold we recommended earlier had the hands in such a position that if you opened them, both palms would be parallel or "square" to the clubface. Nevertheless, if the only way you can hit the ball straight is to adopt a "strong" position of the hands, then do it. It's infinitely preferable to slicing the ball. We can't tell you exactly how far to turn your hands to the right because this will vary from individual to individual, but basically you should move both hands over, as a unit, until the ball goes straight.

Having corrected the slice, you must now correct the "outside-in" swing path.

1. Check your alignment is correct. If you're pulling the ball, nine times out of ten you'll find that this is where your problem lies. Broadly speaking, there are two ways in which you can be misaligned to

the left of the target. In the first, your feet, hips, and shoulders are all aligned to the left of the target. This is the easiest to correct, since in essence you have merely been making a straight shot to the left. Pay particular attention when spreading your feet from the "feet together" position that a line across the toes is parallel to the target line.

In this regard, we might remind you of the "two club" alignment aid we discussed earlier. To use it here, set up to the target normally and put a club down across your toe line. Then go behind the ball, looking down toward the target, and place the other club just outside the ball and parallel to the target line. If you're aiming to the left, this will immediately become apparent to you. If you are misaligned to the left, place the "toe-line" club parallel to the "target-line" club and practice your "countdown" pattern of taking the set, paying particular attention to setting up square to the target line. If you have been setting up too far left, the correct alignment will feel awkward at first—but persevere: It will feel comfortable after a while.

More insidious, and more difficult to spot, is the misalignment in which your feet are square to the target line but your shoulders are aligned to the left. This by itself will cause you to pull the ball because the alignment of the shoulders governs to a large extent the direction of the arm swing. If the shoulders are aligned to the left of target, the arms pull across the ball at impact. To check this, take hold of a club with your hands shoulder distance apart and bring the club up to shoulder level so the left hand touches the left shoulder and the right hand the right shoulder. Now see where the club points. If it points to the left of a line parallel to the target line, then there's your problem. When correcting the shoulder position, check to see that a rigid right arm in the set is not the root of the problem. Also check to see that your ball position is correct; slicers tend to play the ball too far forward-off the left toe instead of off the left heel.

2. Check you have made a full shoulder turn. If you only partially turn your shoulders going back, they will unwind too quickly coming through the ball, pulling arm swing and club to the left of target. A good way to check this is to have a friend position himself behind you, looking down towards the target. If you've made a full shoulder turn, the clubshaft, at the top, should lie in a line parallel to the target line. If it lies on a line pointing to the left of parallel, your shoulder turn was inadequate.

3. Check you have released your whole right side through the ball. If the right side "sticks" on the downswing, your arms will pull across the ball, resulting in an outside-to-inside swing path.

Slice (Type 2). Ball starts straight, then curves to the right.

Here the only problem is the curve to the right. Points to check are the same as in correcting the curve to the right under Type 1: square clubface position in the set, correct hold on the club, and square clubface throughout the swing.

Slice (Type 3). Ball starts to the right of the target line and curves farther to the right.

Agai, the first problem is the curve caused by the open clubface. Consult the three points discussed under Type 1.

Having corrected the slice, you must next correct the path of the swing, which is obviously too far from inside to out, compared to the correct swing path.

1. Check your alignment is correct. If you're pushing the ball, this is the place to begin. As you did in correcting the pull, use the "two club" alignment aid to determine whether your whole body is aligned to the right of target. If your feet check out, use the "club-across-the-shoulders" drill to see whether the shoulders alone are at fault. Actually, when your shoulders are aligned too far to the right of target, it is what could be called a "good golfer's" fault. For it is caused by an exaggeration of the correct set of the shoulders and arms—in other words, you are so conscious of "left arm straight, left shoulder up, right shoulder down, right arm soft and in to the side" that you force the left shoulder too far to the right. However, it is a destructive fault. With your shoulders aligned to the right, the whole arm swing is misdirected to the right of target. Practice taking the set and checking with the "club-across-the-shoulders" drill until you build up a feel of the correct, square shoulder alignment.

   In the same way that pullers tend to lay the ball progressively too far forward in the stance, pushers tend to play the ball progressively too far back in the stance. When you've got yourself lined up correctly, check to see that your ball is off the left heel and not back too far toward the right foot.

2. Check you have not "overturned" the shoulders. (Yes, that may sound as though we have taken leave of our senses, since we said you make a full shoulder turn on every full swing.) We're using the term "overturn" the shoulders here in a specialized sense. What typically happens is that the golfer does not set his right leg slightly inwards in the setup. When the swings back, there is no resistance in the inner thigh muscle of the right leg to the coiling of the upper body. As a result, the hips continue to turn past the 45-degree point that is normal until, at the top of the swing, they have turned almost as much as the shoulders. At the top of the body, this means that the shoulders have turned past their normal full windup position, and the clubshaft will not be on a line parallel to the target line, as it should be, but will point rather to the right of target. If you swing down from that position without making any correction, the path of the swing will be aligned to the right and you will push the ball. Again, a friend can help you to determine whether the clubshaft at the to is in correct position.

3. Check whether you have moved your body past the ball at impact. Remember, we said that there should be a specific "order of movement" in the swing. On the downswing the arm swing should lead, and the release of the right side from the bottom up should time the blade into the ball. However, if you attempt to lead too much with the legs, what usually happens is that you slide laterally with the hips and legs, carrying the upper part of the body with them. By impact, the whole body is ahead of the ball, and the arm swing has,

so to speak, been left behind. The body being ahead of the arm swing, the arms can only swing out to right field, pushing the ball.

Another way in which it is common to "slide" past the ball is also attributable to lack of "right leg set." If you set up with slack legs, you can fall into the habit of sliding the hips to the right on the backswing (this faulty action carries the upper body to the right as well). On the downswing, you slide the hips and upper body to the right as well). On the downswing, you slide the hips and upper body to the left toward the target, and again the body is ahead of the ball at impact, pushing the ball to the right. If you position a friend in front of you and make a few swings, your friend can easily spot this fault for you by the lateral motion back and forth of the head. The correction is basic: Set up properly, paying particular attention to the "leg set," and coil and recoil—don't "slide and slide."

Hook (Type 1). Ball starts to the right of the target line, then curves to the left.

Here the correction of the curve to the left involves correcting the closed clubface in relation to the swing path. To do this, you should:

1. Check the clubface is not set closed in relation to the swing path.
2. Check your hold is not too "strong," which means that both hands are turned too far to the right on the grip. A "strong" hold can lead to the hands returning instinctively to the "square" position at impact, thus closing the blade.

3. Check you are not closing the blade somewhere during the swing. Use the "swing-and-stop" method at the halfway point and at the top of the swing to check that you have not manipulated the blade into a closed position.

In the same way that "pushing" he arms slows the arm swing and leaves the blade open at impact, so can too fast an arm swing close the blade at impact. We hear you say, But I'm supposed to have a fast arm swing! True, but a fast arm swing without a quick enough release from the right side of the downswing will lead to closing the blade. This is why, when you watch the touring pros driving the long ball, you will see them releasing very quickly with the right side. As we've said, it's the release that times the blade into the ball. So, if you have a fast arm swing, you can't afford a "dead" right leg; you'd be hooking all over the place. The correction is obvious: You must work on setting the right leg correctly to begin with and then coiling the upper body around a firm right leg. Then it will release correctly in the downswing and square the blade up at impact.

In the same way that a "slicer" must, as a last resort, go to a "stronger" hold, so a "hooker" should go to a slightly "weaker" hold if the hook persists. You should "weaken" the hold until the hook disappears.

To correct the "push" part of this type of hook, the overly "inside-to-out" swing path, refer to the correction of the relevant portion of the Type 3 slice.

Hook (Type 2). Ball starts straight, then curves to the left.

Here the only problem is the closed clubface. Refer to the relevant portion of Type 1 hook.

Hook (Type 3). Ball starts to the left of the target line and curves farther to the left.

Again, we have already covered the corrections above. To correct the closed clubface, see Type 1 hook. To correct the outside-in swing path, the "pull" part of the action, see the relevant portion of the Type 1 slice.

For the sake of completeness, we'll point out that you can have a pure "pull" or a pure "push". To correct the pure "pull", refer to the relevant portion of the Type 1 slice; to correct the pure "push," refer to the discussion of the Type 3 slice.

THE FOUR FUNDAMENTALS

In the course of the six preceding chapters, we have explained the importance of a true swinging action, we have taught you how to hold the club and set up to the ball, and you have progressed from the miniswing with the 7-iron to the full swing with that club and with the others. We have even offered an advanced course in perfecting the swing. We do believe that any intelligent golfer who follows our instruction will develop a fine, free swing.

However, it's been our experience that many golfers need quick help right now! They need to grasp the underlying fundamentals of the swing that will enable them to work out of a slump or to find a quick correction when out on the course with their golfing worlds collapsing around their ears.

To overcome this problem we developed the Four Fundamentals. These have enabled us to help our pupils quickly and to give them something solid to take home with them in addition to the principles of the true swing. The Four Fundamentals in no way replace the true swinging action; they are, in fact, the four major fundamentals of the swing-and at the same time they are the four major areas in which our pupils' swings tend to go off the track. They are an integral part of the Obitz/Farley system.

Without further ado, the Four Fundamentals are:

1. Alignment
2. Shoulder Turn
3. Tilt
4. Release

You know three of them already, but we will comment on each to put them all in perspective.

Alignment. By now you appreciate the importance of square alignment. We pounded in its importance while discussing the setup, and you have just been through the various types of hooks and slices. However, when working with the Alignment fundamental in your own game, we want you to think of Alignment with a capital A. It's not just the alignment of the feet that is important; for a straight shot to result, the clubface must be square, the hold must be square, and not only the feet, but the hips and shoulders, too, must be squarely aligned. As you've seen, if any of these are misaligned, the swing can be ruined.

An interesting point about clubface alignment is that, by having the clubface square in the set, you're more apt to swing the club on the correct plane.

However, if you inadvertently set the blade open to start with, you can easily fall into a flat roundhouse swing in which you work the arms and the club around the body and open the blade still more on the backswing. Then, of course, you have to close the blade coming through the ball to try to hit it squarely. The opposite applies if you set the blade closed in the set: You'll tend to close the blade even more going back, and you'll tend to swing the arms up on far too upright a plane. On the downswing you again have to compensate by opening the blade, otherwise you'll never hit the ball squarely. Now can you appreciate the virtue of a square clubface in the set?

Shoulder turn. The Shoulder Turn is a full turn of the shoulders on the backswing in response to the upward swing of the arms.

The first point to be made about the Shoulder Turn is that, unless you turn the shoulders with the arms and turn them fully, you're going to be lifting the club with your hands or your arms rather than swinging. If you lift with the hands, you will twist the blade out of a square position, making it difficult to return the blade to the ball squarely and to hit it straight. If you lift with your arms, you're taking the club up too vertically above the plane of the correct swing, and you will probably chop right down into the ground. Without the shoulders responding fully to the arm swing, you can't swing.

The full turn of the shoulders helps to provide proper timing to the swing. If you make a Shoulder Turn, but happen inadvertently to open or close the clubface a little with the hands, the full shoulder turn gives you time to readjust the blade with your hands on the downswing so that you can meet the ball squarely. Without a Shoulder Turn, the action is more rushed, and you don't have the time to make the necessary compensation. The shoulder turn also assures you of the proper weight transference. If you turn the shoulders fully, you know that your weight has shifted with the turn. You're then in position to let your body come into the shot behind the swing to give you all the power you need. If you don't make a full shoulder turn, too much weight is left on the left foot at the top, and you have to force with the arms and hands. When you do that, you're probably going to mishit the ball-or if you do catch it, you won't have a great deal of power.

Tilt. "Tilt" describes the angle the back makes with the ground as you view the golfer from behind, looking down toward the target. We introduced you to Tilt earlier in this book, but only in regard to establishing the correct tilt at address. Now we want to tell you the whole story, which is vital to the proper understanding of the last section of this chapter, in which we deal with topped, thin, and fat shots.

One of the most common faults that we find in the pupils who come to our schools is that they fail to establish the correct tilt in the set. We see several main types of incorrect tilt. The first occurs in the golfers who have been told that they should stand straight up to the ball. These golfers don't tilt forward from the waist at all, and their whole body is set too vertically; this in turn causes a rigid set to the arms as the golfer reaches down for the ball from too great a height. The main problem with this "vertical" tilt is that, because the shoulders rotate at right angles to the spine, the swing plane that it establishes is nearly horizontal to the ground-far too flat, in golfer's parlance. This swing plane would be fine for a baseball swing, where the ball comes at you in the air, but it obviously won't do for the golf ball that lies on the ground in front of you.

The second type of incorrect tilt we see occurs in the golfer who has been told to bend his knees. These people also acquire too vertical a tilt to the back. They think they are making the correct tilt by bending their knees, but in fact they don't tilt forward at all; they just squat down with an excessive bend of the knees, leaving their back vertical. Again, this sets up too flat a swing plane. The third type of tilt problem appears in the golfer who slouches over the ball. This guy bends forward much too far from the waist, letting his shoulders and head drop forward. Generally, such a player is very rigid in the knees; he's still-legged because he has forced the weight of his upper body out over his toes. To counterbalance himself, he is forced to push back his knees and his seat. No golfer can swing from such a locked position. Equally bad, he's bent so far forward that the swing plane he establishes is far too upright to be practical for golf.

The first two golfers, who stood with too vertical a tilt, are going to realize subconsciously, at some point during the swing, that they are swinging on too horizontal a plane. They will then compensate by tilting forward more. In the same way, the third golfer, who tilted forward excessively, will compensate by raising the tilt of the body. But making such moves during the swing-by so doing, you are in effect changing both the axis and the plane of the swing-makes it extremely difficult to catch the ball flush. The reason? It's almost impossible to make an exact compensating move.

This leads to the second important factor about Tilt: You must not only establish the correct tilt in the set, you must maintain that same angle between the back and the ground throughout the swing. If you maintain the correct tilt throughout the swing, you will get the proper shoulder turn and your arms will swing the club up on a perfect plane. Maintain the Tilt properly and you'll rotate the shoulders around the spine correctly. However, don't confuse the two; that rotation around the spine is the result of maintaining the Tilt. Never try to rotate your shoulders around the spine-it won't guarantee that you're going to keep the Tilt, and trying to turn around the spine will freeze the average golfer (it kills his freedom of movement). The thought of maintaining the Tilt will allow the golfer to swing the arms and turn the shoulders freely. If you don't maintain the Tilt, then no sort of consistency of swing can result. This is because the body works up and down, raising and lowering the clubhead as it does so.

· *Release.* Throughout this book, we've emphasized the importance of the right side releasing in the downswing. You release from the bottom up, from the right heel to the right knee to the right hip-and this keeps the uncoiling of the shoulders until last. Then, between the uncoiling of the shoulders and the arm swing you can time the blade into the ball. By releasing the right side you are able to accelerate through the ball; releasing the right side gives you full extension through the ball and gets the weight flowing correctly into the shot.

The one point we have learned in teaching the Release is not to be dogmatic about how you feel it. Everyone will feel the swing a little differently, and the same is true of the Release. Some 50 percent of our pupils find that the thought of letting the right heel rise induces the proper release of the right side, 30 percent feel it as a releasing of the right knee, and 10 percent feel that the hips make the initial move of the lower body in the downswing. The other 10 percent may feel everything from a push of the right foot to a release of the whole right side! So we say use whichever "feel" strikes your fancy. Don't tie yourself up in knots trying for a "feel" which doesn't work for you. The one "must" of the Release is that the right knee must finish pointing forward of the original ball position.

Now that you have absorbed the Four Fundamentals, we would like to return to our consideration of how the ball reacts. We deliberately left two types of flight until last-the high ball and the low ball and the faulty flights related to them: topped shots, skied shots, and so on. You will appreciate our having explained the Four Fundamentals beforehand.

HIGH BALLS, LOW BALLS, TOPPED BALLS, "FAT" BALLS

In studying the trajectory a ball will take—normal, high, or low-it is essential to understand one fact at the very start: A ball goes high or low depending on where you hit it. If you hit the ball on the top half, it's going to fly low.

Let's take this a step further. Basically, too steep an angle of descent into the ball will drive the ball low because you're contacting the ball above centre. And too shallow an angle of descent will drive the ball high because you're contacting the ball below centre.

When individual golfers need to correct faulty height of trajectory, there are always many possible reasons for the problem in each case. Here we find it helpful to divide golfers into two broad categories:

1. The golfer who is striking the ball reasonably well. The only real problem is that the trajectory of the ball is too high or too low.
2. The golfer who is not only getting shots that are too high or too low, but is afflicted as well by such bad mishits as topped balls, "fat" shots, slices, and pulls.

In dealing first with the better golfer, we would specify three main areas to check for both the ball hit too low and the ball hit too high.

If you play the ball too far back toward the right foot you will contact the ball when the clubhead is still descending rather than catch the ball when the clubhead is at the bottom of the arc. This has two effects: You reduce the effective loft of the club and you hit a little more on the top of the ball than usual. So the ball flies lower than normal.

Weight too far forward in the set. You should set up with the weight equally divided between the feet. If you set up with too much weight on the left foot and keep it there during he swing, you will reduce the effective loft on the club and steepen the arc into the ball.

Weight shifted too quickly in the downswing. If the legs make their move too early in the downswing, and too much weight is transferred to the left foot too soon, this will steepen the arc of the downswing. Again, you will contact the ball at a higher point than normal, driving the ball low.

BALL HIT TOO HIGH

Ball too far forward in the stance. When you play the ball forward of the normal position about opposite the left heel, you will contact the ball after the lowest point in the downswing arc. The clubhead is then ascending. This has two effects: You increase the effective loft of the club and you hit a little more on the bottom half of the ball. So the ball flies higher than normal.

Weight too far back in the set. If you set up with more weight on the right foot than on the left, and keep it there during the swing, you will increase the effective loft on the club and contact the ball more on the bottom half.

Weight held back in the downswing. If the right side does not release properly in the downswing, too much weight is left on the right foot through the hitting area. This has the effect of making the downswing arc too shallow. You contact the ball below the equator, driving the ball up.

When you come to the poorer golfer, you find more points to check, but they are all, as you will see, basic points. The problem, essentially, is that the golfer involved has not learned the true swing.

BALL HIT THIN, TOO LOW, OR TOPPED

The tilt. The fundamental most commonly violated with this type of mishit is the Tilt. Either the golfer adopts an incorrect tilt in the set or alters his tilt during the swing. If he sets up with too vertical a tilt and fails to compensate during the swing, he can hit the ball thin, too low, or top it, depending on the severity of the faulty posture adopted. This type of mishit can also be caused by bending forward too much in reaching for the ball or slouching too far over the ball. What can happen then is that the golfer reacts by raising his tilt during the swing.

If the golfer raises his tilt during the swing, and makes no compensation, this type of mishit can occur. However, it could happen that the golfer lowers his tilt during the backswing and reacts by raising it in the downswing. This, too, can cause thin, low, or topped balls. If you're raising your tilt going back, you're "lifting" with the arms or shoulders rather than swinging. And if you're lowering the tilt going back, watch out for increased bending of the knees in the backswing. This is quite common, as it gives a false illusion of power.

Outside-in swing path. If you're swinging outside-to-in through the ball, this steepens the arc of the swing and in turn results in contacting the ball not only on the outside edge (golfer's point of view) but also more on the top side. This will tend to drive the ball low. If you're a golfer who tends to combine pulls with pull-slices and outright topped balls, this is the action you have to correct. (As we've told you, the correct path of the swing is from inside-to-square-to-inside. The correct swing path results in the club contacting the ball when it is travelling parallel to the ground.)

Slide-and-slide swing. We met this type of fault earlier in the chapter; the point we'll make here is that it can also cause you to hit the ball thin or even to top it. If you sway to the right, obviously you move the arc of the swing to the right, too. If you don't compensate exactly in the downswing, a mishit will result. If you don't sway forward enough, the low point of the arc will be behind the ball, and you can catch the top half of the ball, thinning or topping it-or merely sending it low, if you're lucky. If you sway forward too far, you can catch the top part of the ball, driving it low or even smothering it. This is the most unpredictable type of swing because it can cause "fat" shots and shots hit too high as well. Leave swaying to the trees-it's death to a swing!

The reverse weight shift. When you set up with far too much weight on the left foot in a full swing, what usually happens is that you not only keep the weight on the left foot in the backswing, but you bend the left knee more, leaving all the weight on the left foot at the top of the swing. In the downswing you react by shifting the weight to the right foot. As you know, this is exactly the opposite of the correct shift of weight that should take place-hence the name, "reverse weight shift." When you have all the weight on the right foot as you come through the ball, it moves the arc of the swing to the right, or behind the ball. Sometimes the club will hit the ground in back of the ball, bounce up, and strike the top half of the ball, topping or at least hitting it thin. Sometimes you're lucky and "drop kick" the blade into the back of the ball. The ball will then fly quite well, but you will have lost power. More often, you hit in back of the ball and hit it "fat". The point is that if you're hitting mostly "fat" and occasionally thin or top the ball, the "reverse weight shift" can be the cause.

The tilt. The fundamentals most commonly violated are the Tilt and the Release.

As regards the Tilt, an incorrect tilt at address or altering the tilt during the swing can be the cause. If you set up with too vertical a tilt and then compensate by lowering the tilt during the swing, you can get underneath the ball too much, skying it or—more extreme—hitting it "fat." If you bend forward too much or reach for the ball, you put your weight on your toes, and on the downswing the weight often can be thrown farther forward-and you sky the ball or hit it "fat." If you raise the tilt during the swing, you will often become aware of this subconsciously and try to compensate by lowering the tilt in the downswing. If you overdo the compensation, you will sky or hit "fat." If you lower the tilt during the backswing and make no compensation, you can again sky the ball or hit it "fat."

As regards the Release, failure to release the right side in the downswing will force the hands to take over and "flick" the clubhead, resulting in hitting the ball fat or skying it.

Inside-out swing path. In the same way that too outside-to-in a swing path makes the downswing are too steep, too inside-to-out a swing path makes the path of the swing too shallow as it goes through the ball. If you're a golfer who tends to combine pushes with push-hooks and occasional high or "fat" balls of the push or push-hook variety, you need to correct this faulty swing path before you do anything else. Swinging your forearms a bit more vertically (up and down) is your best correction.

Slide-and-slide swing. This faulty swing can cause high or "fat" shots as the result of where you contact the ball. If you compensate only partly for the sway, you can strike the ground behind the ball, hitting it "fat"; if you're a little farther forward, you can catch the lower part of the ball, driving it high. The message is that if you combine thin, topped, "fat," and high balls, the slide-and-slide swing is a good point to check. To stop the slide, turn your shoulders around the upper spine a little sooner.

The reverse weight shift. See the discussion of this topic in the previous section on thin, low, and topped balls. Also not dropping the left shoulder as it turns will help shift the weight smoothly and correctly. One of the biggest reasons why golfers don't progress as they should is that they don't understand why the ball flies straight, crooked, high, or low. How many times have you heard the cry You looked up! to a golfer who has just topped the ball? There's one of the major misconceptions in golf today. You can't really "look up"; the head cannot pull the body away from the ball. Incorrect body action is what moves the head, not the other way around. This is true whether the head moves up, down, or sideways.

We would like to suggest—no, we'll insist—that from this day on you keep a notebook on your own game. Into this notebook should go key thoughts you find useful in maintaining a free swing and—very important—a list of the faults that you tend to make. You will outgrow some faults, but many faults you may never totally overcome. Which particular faults will recur with you? That's anyone's guess, because every golfer is individual. A notebook will provide you with a checklist of regularly recurring faults to consult when your game is off.

Many golfers never really learn the game; they're forever running to the pro for a correction that they should have learned for themselves. Your objective should be to grow in knowledge as a golfer so that when your game goes off you can at least work intelligently with your professional rather than wait helplessly for the magic word.

4

SWING SHOTS

When you mention shotmaking to most people, they think in terms of deliberately hooking and slicing the ball or hitting it high or low. Those things are part of shotmaking, but the words "shotmaking" and "shotmaker" mean a good deal more than that.

The winners, those golfers who not only win tournaments but whose game will stand up to the pressure of winning major titles, have the swing and the rhythm and the tempo which are the result of perfect coordination of the arm swing with the body coil. They can take a little off the ball or put a little more on it, where the run-of-the mill tour player cannot. All the great swingers have been great shotmakers. You don't have to go back to such people as Bobby Jones and Tommy Armour, both fine swingers and fine shotmakers, or even to Ben Hogan, who could make any kind of a shot—low with a fade, high with a draw, you name it! Sam Snead is a great shotmaker, Julius Boros is a great shotmaker, Gene Littler is a great shotmaker, and Don January is a great shotmaker.

If the great swingers are the great shotmakers, the inference should be obvious: You have to learn the swing, the true swinging action, before you can ever be a shotmaker. You have to learn to swing with a good, even tempo before you can learn to vary it. And you have to learn to hit the ball reasonably straight and with good trajectory.

Much of what we will cover in this chapter is advanced golf. You have to be prepared to put in a lot of time on the practice ground in order to master the more difficult shots. But it will be time well spent, for at the end of the trail is your goal: becoming a complete golfer. We'd like to modify that last thought a little—for the phrase "complete golfer," let us substitute "complete swinger." You will find as you progress that you are not so much learning "shots" as you are learning slightly different swings that will create the shots for you. There is a difference, and it is an important one. To vary the normal swing, you in fact land up with an armory of different swings to meet every occasion. If you always think "swing," you will never go far wrong.

Most golfers are far more interested in learning the technique of, say, bending the ball to the right or left than they are in learning to vary the tempo of the swing. That's a pity; varying the tempo is a basic skill, one that you will use every time you're out on the golf course; bending a ball around an obstacle is something you will use only occasionally.

The first point we want to make about the swing tempo is that you never swing with your maximum speed. You'll remember that we told your early in the book that the first thing you must learn is to use only about 80 percent of maximum as your highest speed of swing (or your normal speed of swing, if you prefer). Anything greater than 80 percent will run you the risk of levering, or heaving with the large muscles of the body, and losing the swing.

However, it is apparent that you can use a faster swing off the tee when you have a big target—say, a 50-yard-wide landing area—than when you have to put the ball on a smaller target, such as a green. And you must be even more careful if you have to land the ball on a 15-square-foot area or you're out of business. Golf courses are set up so that the shorter the approach shot you have, the more hazards you will usually encounter. This in turn means you have to be able to control the tempo of your swing in order to get the precision you need. It can make sense, for example, to play an easy 7-iron rather than a hard 8-iron where the target is small.

Another consideration in playing to a green is whether you want the ball to land with plenty of backspin. This is a product of the speed of swing you use. A slower swing than normal will reduce the amount of backspin you put on the ball. Your normal swing tempo which is slightly faster, will put more backspin on the ball.

When you want to vary the tempo of the swing, you have to get back to the basics of swinging. As we've said before, the arms make the swing and the body times the blade into the ball. So when you want to establish a particular tempo on a certain swing, you have to ask yourself, How fast do I want to swing my arms? Once you've established the tempo of the arm swing, the body will respond with the appropriate amount of action to time the swing.

If you want to hit the ball gently, just let the

weight of the arms and the club work in the downswing. Simply let them drop and swing through—and you will get a very soft shot. If you swing the arms a little quicker, you'll get a slightly firmer shot. The best way to practice varying the tempo of the swing is to take one club—preferably the 7-iron in this case—and try to hit the ball different distances with the same length of swing. To do that, of course, you have to vary the tempo.

Now your reaction to all this may well be, Nicklaus can do it and Dave Marr can do it, but isn't that too difficult for me? Yes, it's difficult. And we speak from first-hand experience because we have practised this way ourselves for years. But get out there and start on it! If you become only half as skillful at it as we are, or as Marr or Nicklaus, you'll still be miles ahead of the majority of golfers. And we're speaking not only of amateurs, but professionals as well. We all know the amateur who prides himself on hitting a 160-yard, par 3 hole with a 7-iron! But it's the same with the pros. There are guys out on the tour who think only of hitting the ball hard and square.

When you really become good at varying the tempo of the swing, you can take care of the guys who hawk your bag on a par-3 to see what club you took. You simply take a "soft" swing with a far stronger club than most people would use on the hole—and watch your opponent blink! Sam Snead is a master at this. He will take a 6-iron and hit the ball 130 yards and make sure his "bag-hawking" opponent knows it! Julius Boros can do the same. But perhaps the greatest of them all was Dutch Harrison.

Harry Obitz: Back in the old hustlings days, Dutch

liked to take young guys just coming onto the tour out for a game. He'd say, "Come on, let's play a few holes." And the next thing he'd say would be, "Well, we may as well play for the caddie fee." All he wanted was the $5 for the caddie.

So they would come to a par-3 hole, and it's 160 yards long, and Dutch looks at the hole and says, "Jeez, that looks like a 3-iron." He takes the 3-iron and puts a little soft swing on it and cosies the ball up 10 feet from the hole. Now the young guy doesn't know what to do. He either swings full and barrels right over the green or he holds back on the shot and sends it into the lake. Whatever happened, Dutch had shot your whole swing down—and he had your $5!

HOW TO HOOK AND SLICE

If you had just read the last chapter and understood the principles that govern why a ball in flight will curve to the left or right, and if you asked yourself, How can I do those things deliberately?, you would probably answer in this fashion: That's easy! To hook the ball, all I have to do is align myself to the right of the target so that my swing path is to the right of target, and then set the blade square to the target so that it is closed in relation to the swing path. To slice the ball, I'd just set up left of the target so the swing path is to the left of target, and then set the blade square to the target so that it is open in relation to that swing path. Once I make these adjustments, I can just swing away normally and the ball will hook or slice.

All this is very true. The ball will hook or slice, and this is a valid way to do it. It is also a good place for the less experienced player to experiment with deliberate hooks and slices. However, this is not the only way to do it; you can also work the ball with the swing. To hook the ball with the swing, set up with your alignment to the right of your ultimate target (the point you want the ball to curve back to) but don't change anything else in the set. When you swing back, swing back with the thought that you are going to swing on a slightly flatter plane than normal. When you swing back flatter than normal, your forearms will tend to rotate the club into a slightly open position. Now, as you come through the ball, the forearms will react, closing the blade and putting hook-spin on the ball. In other words, in the backswing you allow your left forearm to roll over your right, and on the downswing you allow the right forearm to roll over the left. The point is that you achieve this forearm rotation simply by swinging a little flatter than normal and allowing the rotation to take place. In this way you are still swinging; you don't have to put sudden moves on the clubhead, moves which you would invariably try to make with the hands, thereby ruining the shot.

To slice the ball, do exactly the opposite. Set up to the left of the ultimate target and swing back on a more upright plane than usual. When you do this, the forearms will react by closing the blade slightly on the backswing. Coming through the ball, they will react the other way and open the blade, putting the desired slice-spin on the ball.

In changing the plane of the swing, the key to putting the club in the right plane is the cocking action of the right arm—the windup action of the right arm in the backswing that we discussed earlier. You do it this way: Suppose you normally swing back to a point over your right shoulder at the top of the swing. To swing back more upright than usual, think of swinging the arms back to a point outside your right shoulder. But the action that permits you to do that is the cocking of the right arm. If you want a more upright swing than usual, you have to let the right arm go farther from the right side at the top of the swing. And if you want a flatter swing, you have to allow the right elbow to stay closer to the right side than usual.

When we talk about making a more upright swing or a flatter swing in order to produce hooks and slices, we are not speaking of radical changes from your normal swing plane, but very subtle changes. For a fade you might swing up with the feel of, say, half an inch closer to the right ear than normal—and perhaps one inch for a slice. The measures would be similar for a draw and a hook. However, because the changes in the swing plane are subtle, you can vary it infinitely; you will be able to feel yourself putting a slightly different swing on the ball.

Here we would like to cite a problem that can occur with the "close or open the blade in the set" school of thought. Remember, if you set the blade in a closed position in the setup, you tend to swing more upright, and if you set it open, you tend to swing flatter. Now, if you apply this to deliberate hooks and slices, what happens? You want to hook the ball, so you set the blade closed. As a result, you could react with a more upright swing. The upright swing, as we've learned, will tend to make you work the blade from closed to open. This can square the blade up again, and instead of the hook you planned for, you may get only a slight draw. The shot you planned with not come off!

The same thing could happen if you try to slice the ball by setting the blade open in the setup. You could react with a flatter swing than normal, work the blade from open to closed, and that slice could turn into a little fade or even a straight shot to the left of target. We should point out, however, that this problem would be most likely to occur with a full swing at your normal tempo, due to the amount of force in the swing. It would not happen, as a rule, with a "soft" swing or with partial swings. There's one pitfall we'd like to warn you about while you're learning to curve the ball with the swing: Don't attempt to open or close the blade with the hands and wrists. Remember, the forearms swing the club—the hands and wrists do nothing, they just go along for the ride. If your forearms are working the blade from open to closed or from closed to open, you're not going to be trying to close or open the blade with the hands and wrists. If you do use your hands and wrists to manipulate the blade, you will destroy the swinging action.

This raises a point. In order for you to learn how to hook a ball, to slice it, or to hit it straight, you have to know what the forearms are doing. You have to be able to feel whether the forearms are working the blade from open to closed (hook) or from closed to open (slice), or if there is no rotation of the forearms either way (straight ball). This is where the hands come into the picture.

You may remember our saying that the only role of the hands in the golf swing was to feel the club. Now we will amplify that a little. When you want to feel what the clubface is doing during the swing (closing, opening, or remaining square), you have to try to feel what the toe of the club is doing. In the backswing, if the toe is moving faster than the heel of the club, you are opening the blade; if the toe is moving slower than the heel, you are closing the blade. In the downswing, if the toe of the club is moving faster than the heel, you are closing the blade; and if the toe is moving slower than the heel, you are opening the blade. If you are hitting the ball straight, you won't feel any opening or closing action at all. These things you have to learn in practice so that the feel for what the blade is doing—and this feel is found in your fingers—becomes part of your repertoire.

Trying to work the ball with the hands and wrists is a fault that is not confined to amateurs. There are many pros out on the tour who never learn the true swing and as a result never learn to work the ball with the swing. We can think of several who have been on the tour for six or seven years and who thunder the ball—hit the ball hard and square and little else—and putt like demons and still don't win. Their problem is that four or five times during a tournament they get into a position where only a real "shot" will do the job—and to make the shot you have to be a swinger. They try to make the shot doesn't come off. That's how they lose the vital strokes that put then back to fourth or fifth place in the tournament. Then they lose confidence, and soon they're settling for a tenth-place finish. They win money, but they're not champions because they're not swingers and they're not shotmakers.

HITTING THE BALL HIGH AND LOW

Our approach to hitting the ball high or low is the

same as that for deliberate hooks and slices. Yes, you can play the ball a little forward in your stance to hit a ball high and back in your stance to hit a low ball. When you play the ball forward, you increase the effective loft on the club; when you play it back, you decrease the effective loft by hooding the club slightly. And yes, putting a little more weight on the left foot in the setup will help you hit the ball low, and more weight than normal on the right foot in the set will help you hit the ball high.

The way you work the ball high or low with the swing ties in with our principle that the arms make the swing and the body times the swing. You don't try to flick the ball up high with the hands, nor do you beat down on it. You do it with the body.

You don't make any changes in your setup to the ball or in the backswing. It's the downswing that does the job. If you want to hit the ball low, you shift your weight a little more quickly than usual to your left side. You allow the right side to release a little earlier, which means the arms swing down a little later and you catch the ball a little later, when the blade is a little more hooded, and you drive the ball low.

The reverse applies to hitting the ball high. Here you start the arms swinging down, but you don't let the right side release until a little later than usual. You keep behind the sot a little longer, keep a little more weight than normal on the right side through the hitting area, and you hold the body back a fraction to let the arms and the club pass in front of you sooner, before the body can close the blade. This causes the club to swing upwards sooner, sending the ball higher than usual.

One thought we would like to add on both hooking and slicing the ball and hitting it high and low is this. Whether you decide to make your adjustments in the set or to make the shot with a special type of swing—work it with the swing, as we described it—it is important that you don't get so hung up on the changes you're making that you forget to swing the club. There's a great tendency to introduce leverage of some kind when you're trying to work the ball. The moral is obvious: You must practice these shots before you can use them. You must have total confidence in your ability to make them out on the course. As Ben Hogan once put it so nicely, Never play a shot you haven't practised recently!

There are many, ways to make the ball curve or to fly high or low. Here we have only been able to scratch the surface. However, we will say this: You can make your adjustments in the set, you can work the ball with the swing, or you can combine the two if you wish. As we said a couple of times earlier, one shouldn't be too dogmatic about golf. Certainly in shotmaking there is more than one road home, and what suits you is what is right for you.

We should also touch on club selection in regard to these various shots. You should take a stronger or weaker club according to the following observations: By and large if you're hooking the ball, you will get more distance than normal out of a club unless you're hooking the ball so much that it flies low to the ground. If you're fading or slicing the ball, then you're going to lose distance (how much distance depends on how much sidespin you put on the ball). When you're hitting high shots and low shots again you must realize that this will affect distance. If you're going to hit a shot low and have a lot of weight on your left foot at impact, you don't have the advantage of your weight being behind the shot (as in a normal swing), so you're going to lose distance. And if you're hitting the ball high, some of the force you generate will be expended by hitting the ball high—and again you will get less distance than normal.

PLAYING TROUBLE SHOTS

Every golfer, even champion golfers, gets into trouble. How well you get out of trouble depends on how accurately you assess the lie and on intelligent club selection. Many golfers panic when they get into the rough; worse, they lose their temper and attempt impossible shots. The first rule of coping with rough is to accept the penalty of less distance and then see what is possible in the circumstances.

If you're lying well, the shot can be played normally. Club selection enters the picture when it is impossible for you to apply the clubface to the ball cleanly. If you know that some grass will come between the clubface and the ball at impact, you know that this will reduce backspin and the ball will come out of the rough somewhat lower and will run more. Thus you should select a slightly weaker club than normal in these circumstances.

The deeper the ball lies in the rough, the more likely it is that the grass will twist blade out of alignment as you swing through the ball. In such circumstances, you must firm up your hold on the club. When you firm up your hold, put more body in the shot—more shoulder action—and release from the right side. This compensates to some degree for the reduced "flailing" action in the wrists resulting from the firmer hold. Really drive that right side through the ball when you're in deep-you'll be surprised how much distance you can get even from a poor lie. If the ball is deep down in lush grass, and you want to avoid having to cut through a foot of grass before hitting the ball, you may find it necessary to set up with a little more weight on the left foot than usual and to break the wrists a little quicker in the backswing. These adjustments enable you to swing down more cleanly on the ball. However, don't make the mistake in such circumstances of lifting with the arms and shoulders and heaving at the ball. Even though you are cocking the wrists a little quicker, you should still emphasize swinging the arms and permitting the shoulders to respond fully to the arm swing. This action will keep the club in front of you at all times despite the quicker wrist break.

UPHILL, DOWNHILL, AND SIDEHILL LIES

These lies are the nemesis of the average golfer. Too often his attitude is one of resentment that he has gotten an uneven lie. Think of these lies instead as a challenge to you as a shotmaker. This will keep your mind where it should be—on the steps necessary for making a good swing from these lies.

Uphill and downhill lies. There are two schools of thought on these lies. One school says that you should try to make your body as perpendicular to the slope as possible. The idea is that you set yourself up to swing parallel to the slope right at the address. However, on anything way to stand to the ball. You feel that you must stand there locked in place—and the tendency is to lose the swing.

We favour bending the uphill knee on these lies in order that the body can be more vertical. When you're standing vertically at address, you're in a more normal and natural position, and you can swing back more freely. On the downhill slope, remember that you have to break the wrists a little more quickly than normal in the backswing. If you don't, you run the risk of the club "sticking" in the hill as you swing back. Don't make the mistake of sitting back on your right leg at the top and trying to "scoop" the ball up; you will only cold-top the ball. Instead, release strongly down the slope, making a special effort to swing the club parallel to the slope. Don't worry if the severity of the slope means you lose your balance in the finish and you have to take a step forward with your right foot to avoid falling over. It's more important to strike the ball cleanly than to have a pretty finish!

Because of the downslope, you effectively reduce the loft of the club you play with. So take a club lofted enough to get the ball up in the air. You'll also find that, because you have to release strongly down the slope in order to contact the ball flush, there's a tendency for the body to get ahead of the ball at impact. This can leave the blade open through the hit, so allow for a push/slice action when setting up to the ball.

On the uphill slope, it's important to kick the right knee in a little more than usual when setting up. There's a tendency from these lies to sway to the right (down the hill) when swinging the club away from the ball. You have to make an extra effort to coil the body in place around the right leg from this lie so that you keep your swing centre steady; the slight extra inward set of the right knee helps you accomplish this. As you swing through the ball, the important point again is to swing the club through parallel to the slope. However, this will inevitably leave more weight than normal on the right leg through the hit. This in turn means that it is very easy to pull/hook the ball. Again, club selection is a factor. Because you are hitting up the slope, you effectively increase the loft on the club, and you expend more force in hitting the ball up rather than along. For this reason, take a stronger club than you normally would for the distance.

Sidehill lies. The chief problem with sidehill lies is retaining one's balance: There's a tendency to fall down the slope during the swing because the force generated in the swing will tend to pull you back on your heels when the ball lies above your feet and forward on your toes when the ball lies below your feet. To counteract this tendency, it's important to put your weight more forward on the balls of your feet when the ball is above you and back on your heels when the ball is below you.

When the ball lies above your feet, you have to set up more erectly to the ball than usual and farther away from it. This has the effect of flattening the swing plane so that the ball will curve to the left in a hooking flight pattern. So the first thing to do is to aim to the right of the target to compensate for this right-to-left flight. However, there is a way of setting up in a slightly more normal position—by choking down on the grip of the club (one inch or so on a moderate slope, more if the slope is severe). This has the effect of enabling you to tilt forward a little more from the waist in the normal fashion. To compensate for the loss of distance you get from choking down (choking down narrows the radius of the swing), you should select a slightly stronger club than usual.

Another consideration in selecting a stronger club is that it's most important not to swing too hard when the ball lies above you. As we said, there's a tendency to fall down the hill, so to speak, during the swing. So a smooth, steady swing with a stronger club will be more helpful than a harder swing with a weaker club. When the ball is below your feet, you have to bend forward more from the waist and reach downward for the ball. This is an unnatural position, but again you can help yourself achieve a more natural position by adjusting your setup. What you should do is select a stronger club than normal for the distance; its extra length will enable you to stand slightly more erect. You should also hold the club as close to the end of the grip as possible without letting the butt of the left hand slip off the grip. The second adjustment is to play the ball closer to your feet.

Whatever you do to make the setup more comfortable, you will still be bending over more than usual from the waist, and this will make the plane of the swing more upright than usual. As a result, you can count on the ball flying in a left-to-right pattern. Accordingly, you should aim a little to the left of the target to compensate.

The watchword during the swing is not to swing too hard. You want to remain steady over the ball in order to make clean contact. One of the best ways to help yourself is to think of maintaining the Tilt on both types of sidehill lies. Obviously, any change in the Tilt during the swing will be disastrous.

The key thought for these uneven lies is not to swing at too fast a tempo. We'll put it even more strongly: Never swing with your full power from these lies. Swing a little "softer" than usual and take plenty of club (except of course on downhill lies), and soon you will find yourself contacting the ball flush and generally enjoying the satisfaction of playing these challenging shots well.

Driving is the real joy of golf, because it's the driver that hits the ball the longest distance. However, although hitting the ball as far as possible is the aim of all beginners, after playing the game properly for some time, players soon realise that accuracy is just as important.

Fortunately the ball may be teed up for a drive, and the height of the teed ball varies according to the driver's face depth. It has been the fashion in recent years to have very shallow woods and irons, but I am pleased to see that designs for the latest woods in particular are returning to deeper or larger heads. With very shallow clubheads, it is too easy to swing right under the ball and 'sky' it.

The ideal driver for a middle-or long-handicap player, is a deep-faced, but fairly lofted club. This gives lots of face to hit the ball with, and lots of loft to help get it airborne. A large head usually breeds confidence too. Many golfers find difficulty in hitting a driver because of the lack of loft on the clubface. Any sensible golf pro can properly advise a player on which club would be suitable, as we all know the problems golfers face. When teeing the ball up, make sure that about half of it is above the top edge of the clubface. This will give it the correct trajectory. Golfers who hook the ball can tee it slightly higher, as a hooked ball usually flies lower.

For a drive, that ball should be teed just opposite the inside of the left foot. Only slight variations should be allowed, as the ball must be struck slightly on the upswing, for a full-blooded drive. Just because a driver hits the longest distance, it does not mean that the player should swing faster, or hit harder. The club itself is larger, which guarantees a wider arc for the swing, and it has less loft than any other club. These two reasons alone make the ball go further than any other golf shot, so do not try to squeeze those extra yards out of the club. Just follow the simple rules I have described in this book and you will be rewarded. A full shoulder turn and a full follow-through are essential.

Wooden club shots from the fairway, or even the light rough, only present a problem to golfers who hook the ball, or those who adopt a 'hooker's grip' (right hand under the shaft, or three or four knuckles showing on the left hand). Only players with a poor hold of the club find fairway woods a problem. Of course, beginners find them difficult, too, and would be well advised to use a number 3 wood from the tee. A number 3 or even 4 wood is easier to use from the tee than the driver and far more consistent. It's worth losing a few yards, when one considers the consistency factor. Confidence plays a large part in golf and the easier you make the game by clever thinking, the sooner you will improve.

Long irons are a favourite with many good players, and invaluable to most professionals, but often a nuisance to less competent golfers. Due to their lack of loft and the small head, naturally, only a shot hit in the middle of the club gives the maximum benefit. Most players find they hit the ball just as far with a 4-iron as they do with a 2-or 3-iron so they prefer to use a number 4 or 5 wood instead. It is important to make a full shoulder turn, and a high arm and club action to hit long irons. The correct arc and angle of the club must be maintained to obtain maximum benefit. A long sweeping action, similar to that for fairway woods produces the best results. A steep, chopping action must be avoided. Mid-irons (5, 6 or 7) are the favourites of most golfers and are usually the clubs that players start learning with. Most professionals teach beginners with a 6- or 7-iron because these clubs have a generous face area and enough loft to get the ball airborne, even if it is not hit from the middle of the clubface. Another reassuring thing about the mid-irons is the comfortable shaft length. A 6- or a 7-iron is a very forgiving club.

As it is important to keep accuracy in mind for these clubs, a three-quarter swing is all that is necessary. A fairly full shoulder turn, with a slightly open stance, keeps the backswing in the correct position and aids a slightly sharper descent of the downswing. The sharper descent enables you to control the ball on landing. When the ball is struck with a descending blow, more backspin is imparted. This is why the ball stops more quickly on landing. This sharper descent is caused by the weight shifting forward and slightly across the target line.

Short iron shots are often the key to good scoring. Accuracy is essential with these shots, as most players hit more of these than any other, whether they be full

8- or 9-iron shots or the most used club in the bag, the pitching wedge. The wedge can be used for shots of up to 110 yards or down to 20 or 30 yards. More shots are saved or lost by using this club than almost any other shot in golf.

Many golfers feel they have to use a scooping action when playing a half wedge or pitch. Nothing is further from the truth. The wedge has up to 55 loft and that is more than enough for any normal short shot. A slightly open stance and a full arm action will loft the ball with great accuracy and consistency. Anyone who learns to use this club well, will be admired by golfers everywhere. Again, use a three-quarter backswing, mainly with the arms, shift the weight to the left side, and completely control the follow-through without forcing it.

5

CHIPPING, PITCHING AND BUNKER PLAY

PUTTING

There are very few hard and fast rules about putting. One point which is essential, however, is to grip the club correctly. Most putters have a flat-fronted grip which encourages the player to set the hands with the palms virtually to the side of the club and the tips of the thumbs down the front. Having set the palms in this way, most professional golfers use a reverse overlap grip with the index finger of the left hand round the outside of the fingers of the right. Any adaptations of this grip perhaps with the index finger of the right hand down the shaft or with the hands separated, should follow this guideline, keeping the right palm behind the putter. The putter should then be set squarely behind the ball, eyes directly over the ball, head virtually horizontal for a short putt which makes it as easy as possible to judge a straight line from the ball to the hole. In theory if he head is slightly inside this line there is a tendency to pull putts to the rest of the game: the feet should be set a comfortable width apart, weight preferably evenly balanced. We really the putter should sit sufficiently upright and be sufficiently short to encourages the wrists to stay firm throughout the stroke. A low hand position with a flat lie putter tends to produce too much wrist action.

With a short putt most good putters prefer to have the feeling of a straight back and through stroke rather than a slight curve. Others, however, maintain that the putter must always move back on a slight curve and through on a slight curve. You cannot say either is right but as a rule for the club golfer the straight back and through approach is easier. Good short putting depends on repetition of a sound stroke, the main rule being to keep the putter moving slowly but accelerating slightly through impact, with a very definite, stationary finish. The head should be kept absolutely still, listening for the ball to drop. The putter should move back and though comparatively low to the ground, if anything low on the backswing and with a very slightly rising stroke through impact. The putter should most definitely no brush the ground as possible without touching it. Good short putting is a combination of reading the green well, setting the putter square to the chosen line and developing a really goods stroke. On fast green there needs to be a subtle combination of speed and direction but direction is as a rule the prime requirement.

With long putting, good results depend far more on excellent judgement of distance. As a rule a player is unlikely to be more than a few inches off the chosen line but can easily leave the ball several feet short or rum it several feet past. The stroke becomes less important, many good long putters letting the hands and wrists come in to play far more to produce good sensitivity and a feel for distance. Where short putting depends on repetition of a stroke, practising long putting should far more be a question of trying to get the strength quickly and easily. With short putting a lot can be achieved by repeating one putt over and over again. With long putting far more is gained by tackling one putt, reading it well and judging the distance thoroughly, and then moving on to a different putt. Long putting is perhaps 99 per cent distance judgement.

GENERAL TECHNIQUE

Developing a routine

Short putting requires a good routine in just the same way as the long game. Here is a guide to a good routine to use. First have two practice swings, making sure that these practice swings are parallel to the line of the putt and not aimed at the hole. Next set the putter behind the ball, ensuring that it is square and sitting flat on the sole. Take up the grip afresh. At this point make sure you just lift the putter clear of the ground to ensure it is in your hands and not resting on the ground. You can set it back again to touch the ground but the putter must always be 100 per cent supported by you can swing it back as slowly and smoothly as you can swing it back as slowly and smoothly as you like. Move the putter straight back and straight through into a perfectly stationary finish, keeping the head absolutely still and listening for the ball to drop. On distances up to at last six feet you will be aware of the ball out of the corner of your left eye and will soon find there is no need to move the head or even move the eyes. Repeat this routine swings for each putt, setting the putter head, lifting it to support it and then repeating the stroke.

Using the sweetspot

The sweetspot of the putter is the point which gives you the most solid, sound hit. If you strike the ball too near the heel it will tend to twist shut. First test your putter to check the sweetspot. The easiest way of doing this is to support the club between the thumb and index finger of your left hand and to tap along the face of the putter, starting at the toe and working towards the heel, with a tee peg or small coin. At first you will feel the putter twisting and then, as you work back towards the centre of the putter face. You will find it no longer seems to twist but wants to move straight back and forward. In this area where not twisting is felt you have the sweetspot. Some putters. Such as the Ping variety or centre-shafted putter are designed to give a maximum sweet spot to keep the ball on line. Hopefully, having assessed the sweetspot, you will find that any line on the putter positioned by the manufacture corresponds with the sweetspot. If there is no line or the two' don't correspond, mark the top of the putter accordingly. You need to strike the ball reliably from the sweetspot and should practice doing so. The first way of checking this is to mark the back of a ball and seeing where it leaves a mark on the clubface. If too much to the left, and if too much towards the toe the chance are the odd one will be pushed. Professional golfers will sometimes try to keep a ball to the left of the hole on a left-to-right putt by striking and conversely with a right to-left putt will sometimes try to keep the ball up to the right by striking it a little more from the toe.

Another sweetspot exercise

Another way of practising striking the ball from the sweetspot of the putter is to take a small square of sticky-back paper from the flap of an envelope, to stick this on the face of the putter in the right place and to hit putts on a practice green, concentrating on striking the ball from this precise spot. You can progressively work at making this sweetspot mark smaller until real accuracy with the strike is found. You can feel quite clearly the difference between striking the ball on the mark of paper or on the face of the putter, though, of course, the eyes should be firmly glued to the back of the ball and the contact fully apparent.

Practising the stroke

Ideally in the short putting stroke the putter should move back and through on a straight line or virtually straight line. One of the best ways of grooving a putting stroke is to practice perhaps with three-to-four foot putts with the shaft of another club set down outside the line of the putt so that the putter head is virtually in contact with this. If there is any tendency for the putter head to move out on the backswing it will strike the shaft of the other club and you can clearly monitor whether the putter has been kept on line both back and though. An alternative exercise is to set down two clubshafts and to practise working the putter between the two. In some ways the inside clubshaft is redundant, the main concern in the putting stroke being that the putter does not move outside on the backswing. Some professionals prefer the first routine and other the second.

Checking for squareness

Bad alignment with short putts causes more problems than almost anything else. Most people do not aim perfectly and will often find it very difficult to get the clubface naturally square to the target. Some putters are undoubtedly easier than others. A putter with a fairly long clubhead will often be easier than a small, Compact one. A putter with a flange at the back with a line or some other marking may again encourage setting the clubface square. At the first sign of any difficulty with short putting, check the squareness of the putter by holding it in what you feel to be the correct position behind the ball and then walking round behind it to check this. There is no harm in actually doing this in play, provided you are very careful not to move the putter and so knock the ball out of position. Frequently in setting the clubface is to practise setting up on some kind of floor surface which has clearly defined right angels marked on it.

Checking your alignment

In order to check your natural lining-up, try this routine with a six-foot putt. Position the ball on a flat part of the green with a tee peg six feet or away. Now behind the ball judge a line from the ball to the tee peg and position a small coin directly on this line approximately 18 inches ahead of the ball. Check from behind that all three look in a straight line. Now adopt your ordinary address position and see whether the three still look in a line. For most people who tend to aim off to the right with putts the three will no longer look in a straight line and the coin will seem displaced to the left, If for example the coin looks an inch to the left. If the odds are you are wanting to aim a good inch to the right of it and so considerable right of the hole. Conversely, if the coin seems to have moved to the right, your tendency is likely to be aim over a spot somewhat left to this. If this is the cases then practise adjusting your head position, bringing the head slightly inside the line or more over the ball to see whether the three begin to look more in line. If adjusting the head makes no difference, you need to practise religiously with this three-point set-up until you can convince yourself what a straight line looks like.

Aiming over a spot

Many players who have difficulty with alignment on short putts like to adopt one of two other techniques for achieving maximum chance of squareness. The first is to choose a spot directly on line with the hole, perhaps six or seven inches ahead of the ball. For many it is far easier to set the putter square to this point rather than to the hole itself. If having tried the three-point test above, you know that you don't naturally see a straight line, you may feel uncomfortably aimed left or right of the hole when aiming over a spot. Here again it takes repetition and possibly hours of practice convincing yourself that spot really is on line with your chosen target, setting the putter square to it and concentrating on a stroke which sets the ball out on target. It means in turn be necessary to have someone else monitoring your putting, checking whether the ball really does start out on line. One of the difficulties with putting is that it is not always apparent why a putt misses. It may be a combination of misreading a putt, mis-striking it from the wrong part of the clubface or a pull stroke which starts it off on line. Frequently you cannot tell yourself and need a second pair of yes to give you correct feedback.

The second way of helping alignment is to position the ball so that the name on the ball is directly on line with the hole. This again can be very helpful or the person who naturally consistently aims off to one side or the other. Once more, having set the ball with is line aiming correctly you may feel most uncomfortable, but you have to trust this and concentrate on starting the ball out on this chosen line.

Keeping the head still

Good putters emphasize keeping the head as still as possible. Practise hitting as series of putts of three to six feet, ensuring that both the head and the eyes stay absolutely still until the ball drops. With putts of this distance it becomes apparent that the ball can still be seen easily from the corner of the left eye and you become aware of whether the ball drops straight in, curves in from one lip or how it misses. There is no need to look up at but more short putts are probably spoiled by coming up on the shot than by anything else. If the head is allowed to move prematurely it is all too easy for the putter head to move prematurely it is all too easy for the putter head to move off line fractionally before impact.

Firm left wrist

Most good putters advocate a firm, high left wrist through impact with short putting. As a rule the aims is to minimize the hand and wrist action to keep the putter head travelling on a straight line. An excellent exercise is to practise short putts of three to four feet with the left hand only, building up strength in the left wrist and encouraging the wrist to stay firm. As a rule a flat-fronted putter grip encourage keeping the hands to the side, left one to the front, and combined with the lie of the putter this will see the left wrist held high. There is a reason behind this, for a high left-wrist position tends to be a firm, locked one. A low left-wrist position produce too much looseness for short putting, through it may in turn give feel for the long putts. Practise with five balls, setting up to each, head still and producing a smooth stroke with the back of the left hand taking the putter head firmly towards the hole.

This movement can also be encouraged by putting an object such as a comb or a pencil through the watch strap on the back of the left hand, so that the left wrist receives a sharp nudge at any unwanted movements.

The push stroke

One of faults if many poor short putters is that they swing the putter too far back and then decelerate in to impact. The stroke must not be one where the backswing is too short or has a tendency to jerk and jab through impact. Ideally the stroke should be slow and controlled both back and through. For those players who have far too long a backswing an excellent exercise is to practise a push stroke for putts of up to two feet six inches. In this you set the putter behind the ball and then just push the ball towards the hole with no backswing all. This encourages the feeling of the putter head moving out towards the hole and should convince the player that the ball can move far enough with virtually no backswing. The stroke is, of course, illegal and only a practice technique. Having practised this on the putting green, you should be able to develop it into a good putting stroke by swinging the putter back a comparatively short distance, rather than having a long loose backswing.

Curing the yips

One of the main reasons for yipping with short putting is in starting off with a jerky takeaway. The general advice to the person who yips is to hold the putter lightly. Unfortunately this often allows the player down on the ground behind the ball with the putter actually supported by the ground. In starting the backswing from this position you would have to gather the putter in to the hands and swing it back all in one movement and this tends to be jerky and out of control. One of the finest exercises for curing the yips is to set the putter behind the ball and then to lift it gently in to the hands, swinging the putter back from position where it is held perhaps a quarter of an inch above the ground at dress. The putter must then be firmly in the player's hands and as a rule can be swung back very smoothly. Another version of this which can help is for the player to lift the putter, to set it in front of the ball and then to return it behind the ball before making the takeaway. This exercise is often thought of as one for helping with alignment but can in fact be an ideal cure for the player who tends to start with a putter wrongly grounded instead of supported in the hands. The player who yips needs the smoothest, slowest possible putting stroke and in addition may find practising with both hands and wrists which encourages smoothness.

Looking at the hole

Some players become almost mesmerized by their putting stroke, failing to watch the ball properly and tending to watch the putter head instead. In practising putting you may as an exercise watch the putter stroke but should always when actually executing a shot concentrate on watching the back of the ball, the putting stroke taking second place. For the player who becomes too concerned about the stroke, a good exercise is to practise putts between two and five feet, looking at the back if the hole rather than watching the ball at all. This soon teaches the player to become more concerned with the hole and with direction rather than analysing the stroke excessively.

Some players who tend to move their heads also advocate this as a stroke to use on the course. There have been one or two good putters who have from time to time hit their short putts while looking at the hole, feeling that it actually encourages a better, more positive stroke and gives reliable short-putting results.

PRACTICE ROUTINES

There are several ways of practising putting, not just developing the technique but bringing in a slightly competitive edge and also simulating various situations on the course. The basic work with short putting should be done on a flat surface, to encourage a good broke, also giving meaningful feedback as to why putts miss. The better the surface you can practise on, the more reliable the stroke you are likely to produce. On the course, however, there would have to be an element of reading the green correctly, judging distance properly and choosing an accurate spot to aim at. The various routines below give some give some ideas for exercises, moving on to some forms of putting competitions for practice sessions.

Reading short putts

Most players need to practise putts of three to four feels as much as possible. If you can reliably hole these you can score well. Having practised from one spot, put six balls round the hole in a circle and move right round the circle holing each in turn. On a flat green this encourages correct aiming. On a hole where there is a slight borrow it gives the advantage of some putts being slightly right to left and the others left to right. You should begin reading the putts accurately to allow correctly for the borrow.

A row of balls

Set a row of balls out from the hole, the closet approximately two feet away and each going back approximately 18 inches. Start with the closest and if you hole this, move on to the second, and again if you hole that, move on to the third so on. As soon as you miss one, return the others to their positions and start again. By the time you get to the fifth or sixth put there should be quite a degree of motivation to hole it. It is a good exercise, giving plenty of repetition of the short putts but a good variety of lengths. Quite often it can takes several minutes before all six balls are holed in their original positions, removing the closest and adding it on the end of the line to give as more difficult task.

Short-putt firmness

Ideally in a short putt the ball should enter the hole fairly firmly. This is particularly necessary if the green is less than perfect. A ball which is slowing down on its last legs tends to start wobbling off line and will take up any imperfections. If the ball misses the hole it should be moving firmly enough to travel a few inches beyond it.

For players who are tentative about short putts and tend to hit them too softly, a good exercise is to stick a tee peg or ball marker just above the can in the lip of the back of the hole, practising hitting the put firmly enough so that it strikes the tee peg and drops in rather than just creeping in the front of the hole.

Short side-hill putts

There are two ways of tackling the short side hill putt. Let's suppose the putt has quite a break from the right. You can either aim, say, three inches to the right and allow the ball to trickle gently in to the right-hand part of the hole or you can hit the ball firmly straight at hole or you can hit the ball firmly straight at the middle of the hole and iron out the borrow. Many goods short putters, like Tom Watson, attack the ball firmly and ram the ball at the back of the hole. Others will take a more tentative approach. Any player lacking confidence with short putting is unlikely to want to attack the putt firmly.

One danger is that players practise on the putting green a firm, aggressive approach and then do completely different on the course, where they become nerves and defensive. There is a time and place for both approaches. In a match-play competition where you have a putt for a half you may as well strike the ball firmly and go for the back of the hole. With a putt for a win you may prefer to be conservative, and in a stroke-play competition you will want the slower putt with more borrow. On the putting green there should be two distinct ways of approaching the short putts. Gives yourself a definite routine of practising some short side-hill putts, first playing a batch of short putts firmly for the back of the hole and then playing another batch with a conservative approach where you concentrate on a combination of line and length.

Aiming for a small target

Some players will come in from a round of golf, having putted well, saying that the hole looked the size of a bucket. A good way of giving out self confidence with putting is to practise to a far smaller target so that the hole then looks comparatively large. There are several way of doing this. A good practise routine for indoors is to practise putting to a matchbox, firstly broad side on and then narrows side on for pin-pointing accuracy.

Start first with short putts of eight to ten feet. Similarly on the putting green put a tee peg in the ground and practise to that. This can then make the hole seem comparatively large and a putt much more inviting. Another way of tackling this, becoming progressively more difficult, is to start with two tee pegs four inches apart, concentrating on getting the ball between them. This can in fact be done with tee peg of the hole to give a really small entrance. This exercise can again be started with short putts of three feet, gradually working up to medium-length ones of eight feet.

Long-putt practice

Long putting is a question of producing perfect feel for distance combined with reading greens accurately. As a rule most players on a practice green do not spend much time in actually reading putts but tend to hit one putt and then simply learn from this is making an adjustment to direction for the next one. They ought to be reading each long putt really accurately and trying to get both distance and direction right the first time. Long putting isn't like short putting where repetition of the stroke is one of the keys to success. It is judgement and feel with long putts. An ideal long-putt practice session is to have the green to yourself and to keep putting to different targets, with different lengths and varying borrows. Each putt needs careful consideration, looking from behind to judge the borrow and then considering the putt from the side to see whether it is ball you can be deceived. The correct routine should then be to have a couple of practice swing, making sure that the putter doesn't brush the ground, possibly looking at the hole rather than down at the grounds as you have these practise swings to feel the sort of distance you are trying to produce. Choose the correct line and make sure you really pinpoint the spot you are aiming at. Then while aiming in the right direction concentrate almost 100 per cent on running the ball the right length rather than being obsessed with the direction. You are likely to be very little out with this but can be many feet out with the judgement of length. If a putt finishes a few inches to the left or right but is the right length it is a good putt. If the line is perfect but the length wrong it is a bad one. Don't then seek to repeat the putt to get it right a second time. That is meaningless. Move on to a new situation and concentrate on judging that one.

Practising different lengths

Spend as much time as possible on a putting green practising long putts of varying lengths. Simply choose a spot on the green, not necessarily a hole, and putt a ball to it.

Practising different lengths

Spend as much time as possible on a putting green practising long putts of varying lengths. Simply choose a spot on the green, not necessarily a hole, and putt a ball to it. Then choose another spot and putt that and then to a third. Just keep working your way all over the green and around the green, working at distance judgement until you can really get it right. If you putt towards a hole and are either short or past the hole, make an assessment in inches of how far short or past you are. Then check whether your judgement of this is right when you go to retrieve the ball. Gradually you will learn to see what distance around the hole looks like. Very often the view is so foreshortened that your judgement is relatively inaccurate. You may think the ball run perhaps two feet past and find it four feet past.

You may think you have left yourself perhaps nine inches short and find it is two-and-a-half feet short. Get used to making a good assessment of the distance round the hole to build up your accuracy and judgement.

Checking your long-putt striking

Very often players will get inconsistent distance with their long putts because they don't strike the ball at the same level. Ideally the putter should strike the back of the ball firmly with the same part of the putter head. The putter should never brush the ground as it travels through but should go through almost as close to the ground a possible. Players who get in consistent length will often catch the odd putt too near the top of the ball and may very occasionally just make contact with the ground. In this way the ball doesn't run a consistent length and the strike needs checking. If you strike the ball accurately with a repetitive action you should be able to look at a target, hit the first ball and then without looking up again hit the second and the third to approximately the same length. In a similar way you should be able to close your eyes and strike three balls, one after another to the same sort of distance. If your length with long putts is poor check first of all whether the striking the ball from the middle of the clubface each time and may need to refer to one of the exercises in short-putting stroke from virtually ground level to assess the accuracy of your strike. If you do have any problems on this line it is essential to use a fairly deep-faced putter where the contact is likely to be consistent. A shallow-faced putter can give too much inaccuracy and variation.

Putting to a string

Long putting centres around good judgement of

distance. Most players become too obsessed with direction and pay insufficient detail to the distance. A good Way of practising long putting is to take a piece of thin sting, make two loops and put a tee peg in either end, pegging this into the ground. Then practise putting from various distances, trying to run the ball as close as possible to the string preferably trying to get it just to run over the string. In this way you begin to see distance as all-important. You may like to imagine this piece of string say nine inches beyond the hole and imagine the ball as close as possible to that length. If you can accurately run the ball to this distance it should give you a sound feeling of a long putt which always reaches the hole, with a chance of dropping but then stops within a very safe return-putt distance.

To give yourself a different from of target you can set the string out in an approximate circle on the green, practising putting the balls into this from various distances. Again this should give you a picture to work with on the course, trying to get the ball to finish in an imaginary circle and therefore within this close range of the hole.

COMPETITIVE PRACTICES

Playing round the putting green

A simple way of practising your putting is to play the nine holes or eighteen holes on yourself anything. Finish off even the shortest of putts. This should give you the feeling of wanting to get the long putts in and yet some good practice with the short ones if your long putts aren't up to standard. Make sure that you read each putt properly. As well as doing this on your own you can of course play either a medal competition against an opponent for added pressure.

Laybacks

Another way of playing round a putting green, either on your own or against an opponent, is to play laybacks and to add a little spice to your short putting. In this situation every time you miss the hole you move the ball back another putter length in the direction of your putt. In other words if you miss the hole by one foot you are going to move it back in that same direction to make it four feet away. You literally continue with this on each hole until the ball is holed out. This means that at some stage you are going to hole a putt of at least three feet or more. You can play this quite simply with a straightforward stroke-play round for your own enjoyment or as a stroke-play competition against an opponent. For good players it can also be another way of playing a few holes on the golf course for a little more competitive edge.

Consecutive successes

Another way of practising putting, particularly of a medium length, is to set a putt of a specific distance, say twice the length of your putter, and to putt ball after ball from this spot, counting the number of consecutive putts you can make before missing one. At this point start again, trying to better your score each time. This can be played in a competitive way at the end of your practice session between players working at a set putt in a five-foot to eight-foot range. This again can emphasize to players, whether or not they are able to stand up to even a small amount of pressure. Frequently, while being watched by others or with a competitive edge, those who perform well in ordinary practice will find the task more difficult.

Long-putt practice

Long putting requires good judgement the first time. One of the best ways of practising putting is on an ordinary green with just one hole, putting from various points on the green, reading each carefully and really making it matter. Spread six balls round a green for fairly long putts and aim first at getting each within the length of your putter from the hole (between 32 inches and three feet). Once you feel you can do this fairly consistently, aim for getting each within the length of the leather-i.e. from the clubhead to the bottom of the grip. There should be a sense of achievement if you can get all six long putts even within the length of the putter shaft and certainly within the length of the leather.

As a competitive exercise this can be adapted for teams of players, again putting pressure on good players to prepare them for a tournament situation. In this case divide the players into two teams, let's say five to a team. Set five putts of varying lengths around the edge of the green. The players are then numbered 1 to 5. Player 1 from each team the second and so on. The player scores four points for his team if he gets the ball in the hole, two if within the length of the leather and one if within the length of the putter. Start this first with three rounds so that for the second and third putts five different putts are chosen or alternatively players move round to attempt a different one from their previous putt. The team with the most points obviously wins. Having tried this with two teams for perhaps three rounds it is then worth adapting this so that for two or three further rounds the scoring system is the same except that if any out is outside the length of the putter from the hole the team immediately loses all its points scored by previous players! This really will have players concentrating, again simulating tournament pressure.

A pairs match

A simple pairs match with a difference is for players to alternate choosing spots around the green for fairly long putts, the player coming closer winning one point. This can be made, for example the best of twenty-one putts.

The length of string

A good competitive practice for the end of a training sessions is to put down a six-foot length of string on the green, pegged into the green with two tees. Players then tackle a long putt with the idea of getting the ball as close as possible to the distance of the piece of string with the proviso that it must pass the string and finish short of some other obstacle, say the flag stick, a further six to eight feet away. Players all put a small amount of money in a kitty, the one who finishes closes to the string taking the kitty; anyone short of the string pays double and anyone hitting the flag stick pays double. Alternatively for younger competitors a small prize can be offered for the one closest to the string with some sort of penalty-say running the length of the practice ground- for any player short of the string or hitting the flag stick.

A team game with long putting

Two pieces of string set out on a green, say four feet apart, can give another way of playing a competitive practice. The players are divided into two teams and have to strike a long putt which finishes between the two lengths of string to score a point for their team. This can be made progressively more difficult by setting the lines of string closer together. This can also be adapted by not just scoring points for a success but losing all the team points for a failure. Once again the competitive side of practice will bring out the best in some players and the worst in others. This way of judging distance to a piece of string is an ideal practice indoors, competitively or on your own. Two pieces of thread about a yard long and say, 18 inches apart can act as quite a reasonable target for distance again varying the distance apart according to the player's standard.

Crazy golf

A good competition, particularly popular with juniors, is to set out a crazy-golf course on the putting green. This requires quite a bit of work from a friendly greenkeeper with a white line marker, but holes can be set out to play as severe doglegs, marking out the perimeter of each hole so that the player has to keep the ball within each out-of-bounds boundary. Any ball going over a white line has to be replayed. This is an excellent way for teaching players really good distance control, for the ball has to be judged carefully into specific spots, combined with holing some very testing short putts. The illustration shows a few examples of holes used. They can provide an excellent means of practice and as well as being fun can build up considerable control and feel.

CHIPPING

Little shots form the edge of the green can be divided into two specific shots, chipping and pitching. Pitching is dealt with in the next section. Chipping is basically a little running shot played with one of the medium irons, where the idea is to loft the ball just a few feet so that it touches down and runs the rest of the way. The ideal club for most players to use is either a 6 or a 7-iron and the feeling of the technique should be as near as possible to that of putting. The main difficulty for the club golfer is in playing the shot with firm enough wrists. The very good golfer will often play this shot almost entirely with the hands and wrists if the lie is good enough but as a general rule it is far better to learn a shot which is similar to putting, the left wrist in particular staying firm through impact. Any player who has a strong grip, with the left hand on the top of the club and the right at all beneath, will usually need to adapt this grip quite definitely for chipping setting the hands far more to the side of the club than for his usual game, with the thumbs a little more down the front and so closer to the ball, keeping the hands and wrists up and forward. The higher the left wrist is kept at address, the firmer the wrist action is likely to be. For the long-handicapped player it is often advisable to feel that the club is balancing well up towards the toe of the club to give good feel and the stroke is more or less like a putting stroke, keeping the elbows fairly well tucked into the body but just swinging the club back and through on a small, saucer-shaped arc. The weight should favour the left foot throughout but the ball should be struck fairly cleanly and not with a pronounced downward blow.

One of the most common mistakes of club golfers is to hold the club in the normal way and simply slide the hands will often then be low with the wrists dropped and this produces an unsuitably wristy action. Most good golfers will execute this shot with both feet turned slightly towards the target, left foot withdraw slightly to produce an open stance, knees out slightly towards the the target but with the shoulders fairly square. This gives a good feel for getting the ball towards the hole in much the same way as one would turn to face the hole if rolling a ball towards it.

In a good chipping stroke the backswing and the throughshwing should be of virtually identical length. The judgment of distance in chipping with a 6 or 7-iron is usually very much like that of putting. If you have a couple of practice swings imagining you have a putter in your hand, you should find that you swing the club back just about the right length. In many situations there is no need to loft the ball right onto the edge of the green. All you need to do is to set it off over any little inaccuracies that are in front of you, but the ball can then still touch down on the apron of the green if smooth enough or on the green itself is the fringe is at all shaggy. The hands should always be kept a little forward in chipping so that the club face is hooded a little-the 7-iron sitting with a loft of perhaps a 5-iron. Learning to use one club really well gives a good general-purpose shot. You only really need to alter this when you need a little more carry in relation to a little less run. At this point you may need to work up to the 8-iron or 9-iron to change the ratio of carry to run, eventually moving up to the pitching wedge or even the sand wedge and on to short pitching.

GENERAL TECHNIQUE

The long-handicapped player first needs to concentrate on keeping the left wrist firm through impact. The fault of the long-handicapped player is usually one of stopping the left wrist just before impact and letting the right hand take over. This is often in an attempt to scoop the ball into the air. For the long-handicapped player the easiest way of developing chipping is to make it as close as possible to putting. It is often better for him to use a square stance, and possibly even adopt the same grips as for a putter, perhaps with a reverse overlap grip or with the right index finger down the back of the club. The club should be balanced up towards its toe, giving the same sort of ;lie as a putter. The player will then often find that he can simply play a few shots with a putter and then a few with a 6 or 7-iron and transfer the feeling from one to the other.

By having the club sitting up in the way the player learns to keep a firm left wrist and begins to experience how easily the ball will rise simply by brushing the ground on which it sits. He can then work at firming up the left wrist even further if necessary by putting a comb or pencil down the back of the left wrist through the watch strap, to alert him if the wrist is allowed to collapse.

Mirroring backswing and throughswing

One of the dangers for the long-handicapped golfer is of swinging too far back with chipping and then slowing down into impact. Ideally backswing and throughswing should be the same length. One of the best ways of learning this is to set some obstacle which limits the length of the backswing and then check the length of the throughswing. You can for example position a practice-ball bag a couple of feet behind the ball, feeling that the backswing must then be short enough to enable you to accurate gently through the ball. The stroke must not be jerky but backswing and throughswing should be virtually the same length. Stop in a stationary position at the end of the swing. This may need someone else monitoring you. One of the best ways is for another player to hold two clubs out, limiting the length of the backswing with one and setting where the limit of the throughghswing should finish with the other.

Using the toe of the club

A golf club is designed to produce power. In the long game you want to hit the ball from the middle of the clubface. In chipping you want to encourage good feel. Frequently you will find that you can produce a much softer feel with chipping if the ball is kept well up towards the toe. This is particularly necessary for players who stand fairly close to the ball and if anything balance the club towards its toe end. Most good golfers usually do this to some extent, often without knowing it. The toe of the club will give a soft feel and often give a much better chance of consistent chipping. Another point to bear in mind is that the ball will often look closer to the toe of the club than it really is. Frequently you find players addressing the ball at what looks like the middle of the clubface to them. When they walk round behind to check it is obvious that the ball is too near the heel of the club. Players who get inconsistent distance chipping often have the ball far too near the heel and the ball springs off from time to time with much too much speed. It may not actually come off the socket but the control is lost.

An excellent way of checking the strike with chipping is to set a row of ten balls, less than an inch apart. Start at one end and work systematically along the row, striking each ball cleanly without touching the next one. Any player who is at all prone to hitting the ball too near the heel of the club will find this almost impossible and will from time to time hit both balls. It will also usually drive home to players just how good and soft the feel from the toe of the club can be. For any player who does from time to time shank the ball with a chip or more likely with a short pitch, this exercise can be adapted to give a better clubface/ ball relation ship and contact.

Learning the little ones

The difficulty most club golfers have with chipping is in being able to control really short chips. Often they simply are not delicate enough with a 6 or 7-iron and find a short shot particularly awkward. Obviously in many situations you would simply putt from just off the edge of the green, but sometimes the grass is a little too long or the surface too wet and a chip is necessary. One of the best ways of learning to chip well is to practice at home on a carpet. The shot should be built up from a tiny one of six to eight feet or so, gradually giving the feeling that you can control a 6 or 7-iron for tiny distances in just the same way as with a putter. Many of the same exercise can then be used, chipping to a matchbox, judging chipping to a length of thread and generally practising good ball control. Tiny shots are the basis of the short game; it is far easier as a rule to build up from a little shot than work down from a longer one. By practising indoors the player is also encouraged to get a really good contact just brushing as lightly as possible the little piece of carpet on which the ball sits, or taking the ball completely cleanly, without any downward attack.. For a long-handicapped player who has difficulty in convincing himself that the ball will rise without any his help, a simple way of learning the chipping contact is to approach these shots as though playing a putt trying to push the ball along the ground with no feeling of trying to make the ball rise. Soon the player becomes aware that the ball automatically lifts and can derive no end of help from short sessions with a 7-iron and putter, making the two feel virtually identical feeling the ball react to both clubs.

A good player's exercise

The good golfer should aim at holing most little chips from off the edge of the green. As a rule we would suggest having the flag out and thinking as positively about short chips as long putts. A good way of building up a feeling for holing the ball with a 7-iron is to practise on the practice for the club golfer who could damage the green. The good player will find it very beneficial. Line up a row of balls on the green itself, the closest about six feet away and the rest going back two feet at a time. Start with the closet and aim to chip this in. Then work back along the row of balls, gradually feeling how easy it his to get the ball in the hole in just the same way as with a putter. What this also encourages is a clean, repetitive contact, emphasizing that the putting contact is not a downward one with a tiny divot but a far cleaner, more sensitive one, sending the ball running as accurately as from the face of a putter. This exercise can be done in a similar way by the handicapped golfer on the carpet at home aiming to a matchbox or some other slightly larger target. Again it builds up a feeling for being able to get the ball in the hole and a good, reliable contact.

Practice routines

Varying the distance in chipping as in long putting is very much a question of developing feel in the hands combined with hours of practice. One element is to get a really good and consistent strike on the ball and the second is then to judge distance in the same way as you would with a putter. It must be done right first time.

One of the best ways of practising chipping is to set yourself up on the edge of the green with four different targets in mind, playing to one target, then to the second, then the third and the fourth. Try to judge these shots correctly and then move on to another spot. Again just keep working at distance till you feel you can get it right first time.

Working to a target

Practise chips of different lengths rather than simply going to the hole on the green you are using. I would suggest learning chipping with a distance of about seven or eight yards. This requires a fairly delicate strike without being too short. If the hole isn't at this length, put down a tee peg or other small object and practise chipping to this. Use five balls and first aim to get all five within the club length. Once you can achieve this, aim at getting all five within the length from the clubhead to the bottom of the grip. Work systematically from one point and when you feel you have mastered that, go on to another. This exercise should give the medium and high-handicapped player a real feeling of being able to control the ball, working at the stroke to get a consistent strike and roll to the shots.

CHIPPING IN

It is important to have a positive feeling about getting the ball in the hole. This is particularly essential for the good player, who should practise chipping with the flag out of the hole for anything up to perhaps 15 yards. Put the flag stick down say five feet behind the hole. Take six good balls and try to get each one in the hole, feeling that each must reach the hole but stop before striking the flag stick. This should begin to produce a really positive feeling, preferably working first with fairly short chips of about five yards and building up to a distance of 15 yards.

Chipping and putting

a good routine is to combine chipping and putting. Position six balls around the green and try to get each down in a chip and one putt. You can either do this with all six balls from the same place or preferably with the chips from a different position. The first is probably more beneficial to the club player and the second to the good golfer. Now there is not only emphasis on getting the ball close but on holing a short put as well. The good golfer in a similar way can work at the number of consecutive chips and one putts he can produce, once more either doing this from the position or varying the shots played. This can be adapted as a head-to-head competition, the first one failing to get down in a chip and putt losing. The way of scoring this obviously needs to vary according to the standard of player and the like hood of failing to get down in a chip and a putt.

COMPETITIVE PRACTICES

A pairs challenge

A head-to-head chipping competition is often a good way of finishing a training session. Players choose in turn the position to chip from the one finishing closer to the hole from each position winning one point. This can be developed with good facilities to extend to chipping, short pitching and bunker shots around a certain green. Players go through, say twenty-one rounds, tossing for who chooses first and from there choosing the positions alternatively. This can be done as a simple head-to-head competition or in a form of knockout for four or eight players.

Chipping to a jack

A good chipping competition is to play a game similar to bowls. Each player has four balls, preferably one using white and the other using yellow, but there can be more than two players. The first one hits a ball of a third colour, say red, which becomes the target. Players then chip to this ball, the idea being to finish as close as possible to it, if necessary knocking the opponent's ball away or knocking the jack (the red ball) into a better position. Players take it in turns to play a ball at the jack, and the one finishing closest after all balls have been played scores one point. If he has two balls closer than his opponents he counts three points, and so on. The first one to reach fifteen points wins. To make this as definite as possible the striking area for playing each shot should give the player approximately two feet leeway so that he can take a slightly different angle towards the jack.

Chipping to a string

Another competitive practice popular with juniors is to chip to a length of string. The one who finishes closest to the string wins unless his ball is short of the string. Anyone finishing short receives some sort of penalty, running the length of the practice ground or some slightly unpleasant task. You can soon distinguish those who would at all costs avoid the forfeit, making sure they don't finish short from those who will go for success and take risks. Again this teaches good distance judgement and really fine control, combined with training a competitive spirit.

A chipping team game

Players are divided into two or three teams of even numbers. Each team is given a chip to play of approximately the same length to a hole, the flag being taken out. One point is scored every time a player gets a ball in the hole. Players have, say four chips each depending on time and the number per team. This can then be adapted with a different scoring system as follows. A player receives four points for getting a ball in the hole, two for being within the length of the leather (clubhead to grip) and one point for being within a club length.

6

GAME EXERCISES AND TECHNIQUE

Usually, the best players have the best techniques, although this does not mean they necessarily have the best looking swings. Especially by women, that a certain lady has a very pretty swing but has a very high handicap. Many children too, look good, or have good-looking swings, but do not play particularly well. There is a very good reason for these observations. Most supple or loose-limbed players. Like women of children, move their bodies and legs in a flowing manner, but actually do not control the movement of the club very well. Hence the good, flowing look—but not necessarily good technique!

Occasionally an uncomfortable or awkward-looking player, like Lee Trevino, comes along to prove the purists wrong. However, Trevino, in the eyes of many professionals, is technically very good. His swing is fairly short, but it is consistent. In other words, he is in full control of his abbreviated movements.

Good technique simply means that the very necessary *body movements* a player has to make during the swing, must coordinate with the arm and club movements. What this means is as follows: the shoulders and hips turn out of the way on the backswing to allow the club and arms to swing upwards; the weight shifts on to the left side on the downswing as the arms swing the club towards the ball; finally, the swing is only completed when the left side (hips and shoulders) turn out of the way and the club and arms are allowed to swing up again to a full follow-through. Only the very best players learn the knack of co-ordinating these most important movements consistently-other players do it occasionally. Co-ordination can, however, be obtained by practice. In saying that, most golfers fall into one of two categories. They either use too much body action, partially on the downswing, or too much body arm action, without shifting their weight correctly. Slicers usually throw their bodies into the shot, leaving the clubhead behind and too open. Players who hook usually do not move the body very much on the downswing but deliver the clubhead early, causing it to close and send the ball flying to the left.

Great players, like Severiano Ballesteros, spend hours trying to obtain the timing of these movements. At any of the major events he can be seen making dozens of practice swings, even during a round. Most of these great players call this 'timing'. In fact it's is the 'feeling' of when to deliver the final hit or acceleration of the club on the downswing. When this technique is achieved the player's confidence grows and success comes naturally.

The correct swing, or a consistent swing, must be achieved before any confidence can last. A good technique can be taught by experienced teachers, providing the pupil is prepared to work at the basic principles. Ben Hogan once said 'Any golfer who is prepared to learn the correct grip, will be rewarded a thousand times over.' This is indeed marvellous advice. Practice is only exercise if you don't have a sound method. Have a picture of the correct swing in your mind when practising and get someone to check your mind occasionally. Any adjustment must be done slowly because it will feel strange. Do these things gradually and learn proper control. Good technique can only be achieved by slowly building up the correct movements. If a slow swing is practised often enough, the proper action will eventually be incorporated into the normal swing.

'Technique' in golf simply means that the golf club is held properly, the stance and posture are not exaggerated, and the club is swing into position at the top of the backswing so that the correct angles are achieved. Thus the sequence is:

1. The club is parallel to the ground with the clubhead inn a neutral position.
2. The shaft is aimed directly at the target.
3. The shoulders and hips are properly turned.

Technique on the downswing combines the right amount of weight shift with the correct square delivery of the all-important clubhead. The follow-through is simply the correct positioning of the body which allows the arms and the club to continue on to a well balances high finish.

Most golfers recognize the great techniques of the top players but lack it themselves because they fail to carry out one or two of the most important fundamentals of the set-up and swing.

THE GRIP

Hand separation

In forming a good grip the right hand needs to take up a particular spread, with the little finger and index finger stretched away from the other two. The little finger hooks around and between the first and second fingers of the left; the right index finger needs to be slightly extended into a triggering position. This spread is often difficult to produce, with a tendency to bunch the fingers of the right hand together, causing a clumsy, insensitive grip. As an exercise simply practise spreading the hand, opening and closing the fingers, and then feel this spread in forming the grip.

Gripping for comfort

The inexperienced golfer often finds difficulty in gripping the club comfortably and yet reasonably quickly. With tennis and other ball games you usually have the racket, stick, bat or whatever in your hands virtually continuously throughout the game. In golf you not only have a whole set of clubs, to master, but have to be able to decide which club to use and then take it out of the bag, make friends with it quickly and feel comfortable and ready to hit within a matter of seconds. For the club golfer this feeling of discomfort with the grip is often the difference between his performance on the range and the course. In practice he gains comfort; in play he has to take out the club afresh. An ideal exercise for the long-handicap player is to keep a club at home and practise forming the grip quickly and easily. Left hand, right hand and feel comfortable immediately. Keep repeating, twenty grips at a time, checking the appearance from time in a mirror, until the hands go on in two movements. If the grip is really good the player should be able to pick up the club, eyes closed, and still get the hands on correctly. The shape of the grip—which isn't completely round—and balance of the clubhead give the hands the feeling for getting the clubface square.

Gripping afresh

The club golfer needs to practise forming the grip. In a lesson or practice session the hands should be set afresh for each shot. The pupil often expects the professional to set up the ball for him and then keep the hands firmly on the club shot after shot. This is invariably a sign of awkwardness in setting the hands. In practice, the long-handicap player often sets the grip and pulls ball after ball towards himself to hit, again without regripping. The player obviously feels unhappy in forming the grip and this often explains why his performance in practice is better than in play.

Avoiding the 'piccolo' grip

Players who are not particularly strong in the hands often tend to let go of the club at the top of the backswing. Sometimes the right hand opens off the left thumb. More commonly the last two fingers of the left hand loosen and lose control. The fault in flight is usually one of fat shots—hitting behind the ball. A good exercise, as well as strengthening the fingers of the left hand, is to put a tee peg or matchstick between the very end of the club and the heel of the left hand, trying to retain this in the hand throughout the swing. Practising squeezing the last two fingers of the left hand to the palm of the hand will strengthen the grip.

Correcting a shifting grip

A common fault is to allow the hands to shift before the start of the backswing or in the take-away. Club golfer and professional alike often start to fidget with the hands, a problem which tends to be accentuated under pressure on the course. Starting the takeaway needs some definite movement to bring everything into action. Often either or both hands are wrongly allowed to turn on the club as the grip loosens or tightens. This needs to be carefully monitored and stopped. The watchful eye of a golfing companion and saying 'Stop' when the fidgeting starts is one cure. Another is to set up a row of four balls, six or so inches apart, starting to hit from one end of the row and working to the other without allowing the hands to move on the club. If the grip remains constant, the last shot will feel as comfortable as the first. If the grip slips, hitting all four without an adjustment is virtually impossible. Repeat the exercise until the hands stay in place. At first the hands may have to hold quite tightly to achieve this consistency. For good golfers and those with any tendency to slice, gradually try to achieve the same but with a lighter and more sensitive grip. It is also an ideal exercise for practising watching the ball well through impact.

THE SET-UP

Aiming over a spot

Aiming incorrectly can cause all kinds of directional problems. Ideally the player should see a straight line from the ball to the hole and stand parallel to this, with the entire body from feet to shoulders and the line of the eyes, set on the parallel line. This straight line is often hard to judge when viewed from the side of the ball.

The best way of aiming reliably is to get used to setting the club to the right of the ball, walking behind it and looking at the shot along the line rather than from the left of the ball. Stand about three or four feet behind the ball and look at the target, choosing a spot on the ground about 15 to 18 inches ahead of the ball and on line with your target. Now walk round to address the ball, keeping this spot firmly in mind. Set the clubface square to this line rather than to the flag in the distance, stand with your feet together at right angles to this imaginary line from ball to spot, place the feet apart systematically, left foot first, then the right, and adopt the parallel line. Then trust yourself to hit out over this spot. If you look up at the target again, resist any temptation to move the feet or to realign the shoulders. Practise choosing the spot and your lining-up routine until it becomes second nature.

Practising alignment

At the first sign of any directional problems with your shots, check the alignment of your feet. Set a club down along your toes and view this from behind. The club should not point at your target but *parallel to* the proposed line of flight. If you check this before hitting the ball it is easy to see the line you hope the ball would fly on. If checking after the ball has gone it is worth setting another club down to form the parallel line. As part of your practice routine aim to different targets and check your alignment with a club. Either hit the ball to your various targets and monitor the results, or simply see it as an exercise to practise aiming—an exercise you can easily use in the fairly confined space of a garden. On the practice ground choose five different targets and hit to these at random, making your aiming routine crucial and simulating the novelty of each shot in a round.

Monitoring the ball position

The ideal ball position varies from one player to another. As a guideline the stronger and better a player, the further to the left he is likely to be able to play the ball. Older players and most women need to play the ball further back. The ball is played furthest to the left with a driver to encourage an upward, sweeping attack, and further to the right in the stance, the shorter the club and worse the lie, to encourage a more downward attack. Having decided on the ideal ball position it is by no means easy to keep it consistent. Good golfers have more problems arising from the set-up and in particular the ball position than from almost anything else. It is difficult to look down at your own ball position and judge it accurately.

One of the best ways to check the ball position is to set one clubshaft down along your toes and the other at right angles across this towards the ball to see the precise position of the ball in relation to the feet. The results are often quite different from what the player imagines. This may immediately indicate if there is an error—for the club golfer more often than not that the ball is too far forward, i.e. to the left.

But frequently it is hard to find a comfortable position and the feeling one week may be quite different the next. An ideal way of monitoring the ball position is to check it when things are going well and to keep a definite record of the position. When the feeling is good, stand on a large sheet of newspaper or wallpaper, marking the spot where the ball would be and your foot position. Label the paper with the club used and put it away for future reference in times of difficulty.

Distance from the ball—precise measuring

As a simple guideline, the closer you can stand to the ball the better. Good players are unlikely to stand too close for long without feeling uncomfortable. High-handicap players can stand in close providing they adopt the correct posture, sticking the bottom out to get the body out of the way. But it is all too common to stand too far from the ball, good players often coming to grief by stretching further from the ball when things are going well and just edging too far away for safety. Like the ball position, distance from the ball needs constant reviewing and is hard to check oneself. The newspaper exercise above is ideal for this too.

The good golfer needs to aim for precision and should measure and record distance from the ball with a tape measure or ruler during a spell of playing well, using the driver and 5-iron for reference. An error of an odd inch can throw out the arc of the club through impact to the point where direction becomes erratic. Another way of measuring the exact distance is to set the club on the ground from the ball to the line of your feet, end of the hosel by the ball, and to mark with tape or waterproof ink the distance of your toes from the ball. It is, of course, a reference which must not be used in actual play.

Distance from the ball—visual guide

In play you need to keep your distance from the ball as constant as possible without being able to take precise measurements. This has to be a question of feel. The distance of the right elbow from the body can act as a guide. The feeling of balance on the feet can be another. One way in which you can assess the distance and encourage a consistent set-up is to look at the position of your hands in relation to the chin. With the ball in fairly close, the hands, should feel to be under the chin rather than under the forehead. But what you will also see is the visual relationship of your hands to your toes. If standing in you may feel that your right index finger appears roughly level with the feet; you may feel the hands always appear outside the line of the feet. Make a mental or written note of the appearance of this relationship, again while playing well, for future reference.

The posture in the set-up tends to dictate the plane of swing, the way in which arms and body move in the backswing and the use of the legs in the throughswing. Club golfers, advised to adopt a position like one of sitting on a shooting stick, tend to sag at the knees and consequently droop in the back into a stance which lacks power. The correct feeling in the set-up should be one of standing up tall, pushing the hips back and up as though lifted from the back trouser pockets, and only with the bottom out and up in this way to flex the knees. With the bottom sticking out the arms are able to hang loosely, hands below the chin, wrists dropped slightly.

An excellent way of checking and improving the posture is to stand with the heels about four inches from a wall, pushing the bottom out and up to touch the wall as high as possible. From there, slide the bottom a couple of inches down the wall as the knees flex. This is quite different from the wrong, sagging posture, where the player could stand with the heels against the wall and just slide down it into a powerless position.

Relaxation at address

There should be a feeling of relaxation at address, particularly in the arms and shoulders. The correct feeling should be of the arms hanging loosely downward to the sides of the body, shoulders down—almost forced down—rather than the shoulders coming up and forward with the arms out from the body as though over the chest. To produce the correct feeling in the arms and shoulders, stand up erect and have the feeling from a tall position of forcing the shoulders down, not forward, trying to stretch the arms down to have the hands as low as possible to your sides. Compare this in a mirror with the incorrect feeling of the shoulders lifting, where tension would show, collarbone rising. In this way the hands can seem to be held low at address without any feeling of slouching in the back and shoulders, and the posture encourages a good grip, fingers almost along the club. With the arms hanging to the side, bend from the top of the legs until the hands can be brought together under the chin with the arms still feeling loose.

The right shoulder position

One of the hardest parts of the set-up for the club golfer is to have the feeling of comfort with the right shoulder below the left. The right hand is below the left on the club. One of two things follow from this. Either the right hand tends to pull the right shoulder forward—this is wrong—or the right shoulder drops neatly below the left—this is correct. Achieving this isn't always easy. It is not a question of having the weight on the right foot, nor of feeling that the left hip is pushed out, body arching sideways. It should simply be a feeling of compressing the right side of the body from hip to shoulder and if anything stretching the left. Men with a long back tend to find this easy while women with shorter backs or people with stiffness in the back often find it unnatural. It is an essential part of the set-up. Without it there is a tendency for the right shoulder to ride too high, encouraging a steep swing and aggravating any likelihood of slicing. A very simple loosening exercise is to stand erect, feet apart, sliding the right hand down the right leg without tipping the hips. Right side compresses, left side stretches. Having produced this feeling, bend from the hips to feel it in relation to the address position.

Squareness of the shoulders

It is often hard to keep the shoulders feeling square and comfortable. For many players the right shoulder often feels dominant at address. This will frequently happen if the player is too far from the ball and or the ball too far forward to the left. The easiest way of checking this is to practise with, say, a 5-iron, playing the ball in varying ball positions until the right shoulder feels square. The further back the ball is played, the easier this may feel.

THE BACKSWING

The feeling of the backswing for the average club golfer usually needs to be one of combining a turn of the left side of the body followed by a lifting of the arms. The first stage to this is to turn from the left shoulder, bringing the club back fairly low until roughly level with the legs. If the shoulders turn correctly and with a suitable grip, the toe of the club should be pointing virtually upwards, the club knee to hip high. From this position the hands and wrists can naturally hinge upwards to form a simple backswing. As a practice routine the beginner needs to practise this first stage, toe up and then hinging up with the wrists to a point where the thumbs, and in particular the left thumb, support the club at the top of the backswing, wrists cocked.

Perfecting the plane

In an ideal backswing the shoulders should turn, with the angle of the left arm above the plane of the shoulders. One of the most common errors for club golfers is to adopt too steep a plane with the shoulders, so that the left shoulder drops in the backswing. This tends to result in the right hand and arm being too dominant at the top of the backswing, encouraging an out-to-in attack and aggravating any tendency to slice the ball, sky drives and lose power generally. There are two ways of lifting the hands to the top of the backswing. One is to make the club rise by dropping the left shoulder; this is quite wrong. The other, which is correct, is to have the feeling of turning the shoulders and lifting the arms. One of the difficulties of golf is that the ball sits on the ground and the ground gets in the way. Many players' way round this is to life the club unsuitably in the backswing to produce a feeling of getting down into it again.

In the wrong position the left shoulder drops and the player has the feeling of looking several inches beyond the shoulder down to the ball. In the correct position the shoulder turns rather than lifts, and the ball will appear only just visible above the shoulder as you view it from the top of the backswing. The *feeling* will almost be that the left shoulder lifts rather than drops—in fact it stays virtually level—and that the club is lifted by the left arm and not forced up by the shoulder dropping. The left shoulder covers the chin (and almost the mouth); never let the chin protrude above the shoulder. To produce the correct feeling repeat the backswing, twenty swings in succession, feeling a two-piece action of turning the left shoulder and lifting the left arm, feeling the left shoulder covering the chin and ensuring that the ball is only just visible above the shoulder. If you overdo it you will lose sight of the ball. The exercise is generally easier the longer the club, for the extra length tends to encourage a flatter plane and discourage the steep one. Once the backswing begins to take shape, add the down and throughswing, first without the ball, swinging under the left shoulder but with no feeling of forcing the right shoulder down.

The right arm

In the correct plane of backswing the right arm should fold away to form a virtual right angle, elbow pointing down. A good, old-fashioned exercise is to practise swinging to the top of the backswing with a golf ball lodged under the right armpit. This necessitates keeping the right arm folding in and not flapping out. It is perhaps slightly exaggerated in producing a rather cramped swing if followed too religiously, but is good for encouraging the correct feel to the plane.

Carrying a tray

Another way of feeling the correct right hand and arm position at the top of the backswing is to adopt a position like a waiter carrying a tray. This again sees the elbow forming a right angle, right wrist folded back on itself.

Left-arm dominance

Ideally the backswing should feel dominated by the left side. The left shoulder makes the turn rather than the right. One would think turning the left shoulder or right shoulder would produce the same effect but they do not. With the left shoulder in control of the turn the shoulders stay rounded in together. With the right shoulder making the turn the shoulders and chest open and the right elbow may fly out from the body. Practising left-arm control is one of the finest exercises. As a starting point repeat the backswing twenty times, feeling the left arm to be in control, taking the right hand off the club at the top of the swing to feel the left thumb in a supporting role under the shaft of the club. Once the left thumb feels as if it is supporting the club, practise the backswing with the left hand only, starting from a stationary position at address, lifting it smoothly away to a firms, controlled backswing. Pause for a moment and then return smoothly to a stationary set-up.

Left-arm strengthening

To strengthen the left arm, swing the club to the top of the backswing, left arm only. Now bounce the club up and down 10 to 12 inches, feeling the arm and hand fully in control.

The left wrist

Once at the top of the backswing with the left arm only, practise hinging the wrist over and back, building this up to twenty or thirty twists. This gradually builds up the left wrist, helping to produce the flattish left wrist which usually accompanies a good backswing.

The left arm position

Ideally the left arm should stay straight in the backswing. This gives a degree of extension and encourages a repetitive position. Some golfers find it almost impossible to keep the arm straight. The correct feeling of a really tightly coiled backswing should be one of drawing the left arm across the chest towards the right shoulder, the arm always at a slightly higher angle than the plane of the shoulders. In a perfectly orthodox backswing position the left arm is drawn close to the right shoulder. The club golfer often tries to achieve this without being physically able to, either because of tightness in the back of the left arm and shoulder or through a heavily built upper chest. To produce the correct feeling in the left arm and develop looseness, hold the left arm straight out in front, palm down put the right hand behind the left elbow and ease the arm across the chest towards the shoulder. The player who keeps a good, straight left arm in the backswing will generally be able to ease the arm to the right shoulder, keeping it perfectly straight. The player who feels the movement restricted in the exercise will need to make allowances in the golf swing, either coming to terms with an arm that bends, or having to turn the shoulders more to get the left arm into suitable position for the downswing. Practising the movement without a club, right hand assisting to ease it across, will gradually loosen the back of the left upper arm. Moving the arm unaided from fully left to fully right and towards the right shoulder will encourage the feeling of the left arm movement in the swing. Bend into a semi-address position, without a club, and move the left arm alone from in front to the right shoulder, letting the palm of the hand turn to simulate the backswing.

Developing the wrist action

For the fairly advanced player the wrist cock is no longer an upward hinging of the wrists. Instead the right wrist should hinge back on itself in the tray-carrying position. To encourage this correct wrist cock, build in a couple of backward waggles before the takeaway, hinging the right wrist back on itself, arms staying virtually motionless. The club should travel back in a low, shallow curve in this waggle. Practise this backward hinging as a separate exercise, loose wrists, to encourage the correct inside takeaway. The correct takeaway, following a waggle, in turn encourages an attack from the inside, with the club coming from behind the player and *not* straight down the line of the shot.

Avoiding an overswing

Women golfers in particular are often worried by an overswing, the club shaft being well beyond the horizontal at the top of the backswing. This can happen through the player being extremely supple (which causes little problem) or from a loosening grip, a bending left arm or from a late wrist cock. Whatever the cause, the result is usually loss of power and a tendency to hit behind the ball. The club golfer will often overswing because of trying to copy the look of professional golfers and confusing appearance and feel. Professional golfers usually seem to have a wide, stretched backswing, with the wrists seeming to cock at about hip or waist height. The player copies what he thinks happens and will often swing back to what feels like waist height before bringing the hands into play. The wrist cock then happens too late in the swing, with the arms above the head and the hands and wrists dropping unsuitably. What the professional golfer usually does is to feel that the hands are active right from the moment of the takeaway, wrists beginning to cock as the arms start their swing.

An exercise for shortening the swing is to practise with a 6 or 7-iron, cocking the wrists as early as possible on the backswing (and throughswing) to shorten the swing for a crisp, punchy shot. The player is usually surprised at the length and power achieved and can gradually adapt the feeling to the longer clubs.

Curing a locked right leg

In the backswing the shoulders, and to a lesser extent the hips, should turn to produce the correct direction to backswing and downswing. For players who need a fairly large hip turn, particularly women and older men, there is a danger of the right leg straightening and the knee locking back. This usually immobilizes the legs in the start of the downswing. To correct this it is first necessary to adopt the correct foot position at address. The feet need to be set with the outsides of the feet outside the width of the shoulders *and hips*. This means that the hip and leg turn is more easily contained within the width of the stance without any tendency to roll onto the outside of the right foot. The weight should be concentrated towards the inside of the right foot, feeling it pressing down on the inside of the foot, while transferring the weight correctly in the backswing. An exercise to encourage the correct feeling is to stand with a golf ball or clubshaft under the outside of the right foot at address, forcing the weight onto the inside of the foot. Turn and swing to the top of the backswing, feeling that weight transfers towards the right feeling that weight transfers towards the right side in turning, but still feeling pressure on the inside of the foot. As a rule this feeling of staying on the inside of the foot. As a rule this feeling of staying on the inside of the foot combined with a turn stops the right leg locking and keeps the knee flexed in readiness for moving well through the ball by impact.

CONTACT PROBLEMS

Playing good golf requires a sound contact with the ball. It is perhaps the only ball game where the contact with the ball is difficult. The ball is small, the clubhead is small and the ball sits on the ground—the ground gets in the way. The long-handicap golfer often labours under the misapprehension that if the swing looks reasonably correct the club will strike the ball soundly. Sadly this just isn't so. Striking the ball from the middle of the club with the right depth of contact requires a trained eye or very natural ball sense combined with an ability to watch the ball well to the moment of impact. This section of exercises is largely aimed at the beginner and long-handicap golfer, but with ideas for the experienced player who suffers occasional disastrous shots.

Learning the contact

The beginner often finds difficulty in transferring his practice swing to the ball because of its small size and the precision required. The general tendency is to try to lift the ball into the air, falling back on the right foot and in so doing catching the ground. An ideal way of learning, particularly for those who are not gifted games players, is to learn with a tennis ball or a light plastic ball that size. The extra size means that the player can more easily get the feeling of striking the ball below its centre, getting the ball to rise quite easily without any urge to scoop it up. Once the swing can be reasonably grooved with the larger ball, the next stage is to try with a smaller light ball or to progress to a golf ball, teeing it up on a low peg to instill confidence. The tee can then be lowered or removed altogether, at first sitting the ball on a tuft of grass to make the contact easier. This feeling for the depth of contact is very hard for many players and needs to be acquired systematically. If the player tries to hit a golf ball from bare ground as a beginner, he will usually find the contact so difficult that the swing itself is seen as being too complex and the natural swing can all too easily disappear. Using this exercise the player gradually improves the depth judgement without becoming obsessed with the swing.

Sweeping the fairway woods

The ideal contact with a fairway wood is to brush the ground on which the ball sits. Providing the whole ball sits above the ground, without settling in a depression, there is no need to strike it on the downswing. The sweeping contact produces good height and encourages maximum length. The depth of contact needs to be judged very finely, the barer the lie the more accurate the depth needs to be. It is important with these shots to produce practice swings where the sole of the clubhead brushes the ground—not just tickling the grass, but with the sole plate bouncing on the ground. On firm ground there should be a definite sound as the club bounces. One of the ways of practising this is to use a rubber driving-range mat, feeling the bouncing contact and gradually monitoring this until the contact is in precisely the right spot. The player will benefit from thinking of the sole plate on the bottom of the wood and of bouncing this onto the ground directly behind the ball, almost with a feeling of slapping it down behind the ball and drawing it up again beyond impact. In learning to play good fairway woods, try initially from a very low tee, just setting the ball a fraction off the ground, and then reproduce the same feeling from increasingly bare lies, until good depth judgement is learned.

Watching the ball

The professional golfer can usually get away with looking away from the ball momentarily before impact, but will from time to time have to concentrate on watching it really well to produce a perfect strike. This is particularly the case from any bare or bad lie. The long-handicap player whose swing is less grooved certainly needs to look at the ball until the moment the ball is struck, being conscious of staying looking down and seeing the grass for a split second after the ball has gone, and yet completing the swing through to follow the flight of the ball. Many golfers find it almost impossible to stay with the ball long enough and have an irresistible urge to look up early. A way of practising the feeling of being able to watch the ball well is to hit a row of four balls, addressing each, hitting each and then looking at the next rather than following the flight of the previous one. The correct way of doing the exercise is to swing through to a full finish with each shot, holding it for a second or so before turning to the next, but still without following the flight. The player is gradually able to watch the ball well and complete the swing in an uninhibited way.

In watching the ball the eyes should focus on the back of the ball—the part the clubface is going to hit—rather than looking down at the ball as a whole or on its top. In practice or for the drive it is well worth setting the ball with the maker's name or number on the back to give some extra focal point, a coloured blob of ink acting as a definite reminder for players continually fighting the urge to look up too soon.

Checking the divot

Ideally in striking an iron shot the ball should be contacted slightly on the downswing, with the clubhead continuing through to take a divot. The divot should start as near as possible below the middle or front edge of the ball. Players who watch the ball well through impact are usually aware of their divots, knowing the feeling of crispness and perfect judgement. Longer-handicap players often mis-strike the ball by coming down too far behind the ball or too far ahead of it. Watching the divot and monitoring its precise position in relation to the ball can give feedback for making improvements. To assess the precise position of the divot and whether the contact is correct, put in a tee a couple of inches outside the middle of the ball. After hitting the ball, note the position of the back of the divot telling you quite simply whether there has been a tendency to hit the ball heavy or thin. The good golfer can feel the difference. The club golfer may not be aware of the exactness of the contact without this kind of proof.

Positioning on the clubface

It is essential to hit the ball from as near as possible to the middle of the clubface. Long-handicap players often produce an inconsistent contact, striking the ball almost at random from various parts of the clubface. Good players will usually produce a consistent strike but may find their shots creeping slightly towards toe or heel without necessarily knowing why the strike feels less than perfect. It is important to address the ball from the centre of the clubface. This sounds simple but isn't always straight forward. In looking down at the clubhead from the address there is frequently an optical illusion in that the ball viewed from this position and seeming to be central on the face is often further towards the heel than the player imagines. It is therefore worth checking the ball/clubface position from behind the club and ball. To make yourself aware of the centre of the face it is worth practising with a small piece of sticky paper (from the flap of an envelope for example) on the sweetspot of the clubface. But even with the ball addressed centrally on the clubface there is no guarantee that the strike will be perfect.

An exercise for checking the strike is to put a small blob of lipstick, chalk or coloured marker on the back of the ball, to strike it and then see where the telltale mark is left on the clubface. Long-handicap players may be surprised at the discrepancy in the results; top-class golfers can sometimes find themselves a fraction too near toe or heel for comfort. Having assessed the pattern of strike the long-handicap golfer will usually find improvement simply by repeating the exercise, perhaps hitting into a net, concentrating on the feeling and sound of connecting with the ball accurately and checking the feedback from the marks on the clubface. The low-handicap player will usually be able to rectify the errors simply by thinking in terms of the clubface contact, edging the ball back towards the sweetspot.

Curing a shank

One of the most devastating shots in golf is the shank or socket—the ball flying off the bottom of the shaft. Long-handicap players who produce these shots often do not know whether the ball has been struck from the end of the toe or from the socket. Both fly off to the right, of course, and although the feeling is quite different they are not necessarily able to distinguish one from the other. The first point is to be certain what the shot is. A simple way of checking the contact, and indeed to set about correcting it, is to address the ball with another ball or tee about an inch outside the target one. The player who sockets is likely to bring the club down too far from his feet and to catch both balls, often sending the outside one away more satisfactorily than the inside one. This feedback is often sufficient to enable him to cure the problem, concentrating on swinging the club through on the right path.

The socket is a common shot and once the player does a few it is a fault that tends to worsen. There are several reasons for shanking, but looking at the contact initially often helps the player. The socket may simply arise because the player swings the clubshaft, which is in effect an extension of the arms, rather than appreciating that the clubhead is extended out from this. The player may need to think hard of striking the ball from towards the toe, and even practise setting up to the ball and then deliberately swinging down and missing it on the inside to find judgement and control of the path the clubhead takes. Commonly players socket because of bad balance through impact, falling forward onto the balls of both feet through impact and so bringing the club toppling forward slightly rather than, as the player usually assumes, standing in too close. This kind of socket can be cured most easily from a combination of good balance in the finish, emphasis being on the left heel through impact, and working on the two-ball exercise set out above.

Players who socket the ball from bad balance are often prone to hitting wood shots from the heel of the club, with the odd disaster which flies straight left. Again the beginner doesn't necessarily understand why the irons shoot off to the right and the woods to the left.

Shots from the toe

Hitting the ball from the toe is less common than the socket, but if the ball comes off the every end of the club it can be just as devastating. A good exercise for trying to correct shots from the toe is to place a tee peg a quarter of an inch or so outside the ball, with the idea that if the ball is struck from the middle of the club, the tee peg will be collected too. By careful positioning of the tee it is easy to get good feedback of what is happening through impact. Players who do hit the ball from the toe, and indeed those who tend to socket, produce these errors in practice swings as well as with the ball. Often they will exclaim 'I can do it without the ball' and yet the odd inch error through impact shows clearly. The fault is often closely allied to topping the ball, with a tendency to pull the arms in and up through impact instead of stretching and extending.

The upward driver contact

Hitting a teed-up ball with a driver requires a different contact from the fairway woods and irons. The ball, because it sits above the ground, can be struck on the upswing, giving maximum chance to produce clubhead speed and a penetrating trajectory. To help produce this upward contact, the ball is positioned well forward in the feet, perhaps an inch or so inside the left heel. The feeling, however, must be of keeping the weight fairly central in the feet and so behind the ball.

Players often have considerable difficulty in producing an upward contact with a driver, having mastered the downward or sweeping contact with the other clubs. Frequently there is a tendency to play the ball forward but then to sway to the left through impact, imparting a downward blow onto the ball. This tends to lead to striking it from the top of the clubhead, so that the ball takes off with excessive height. The correct feeling should be that the bottom of the swing skims the ground several inches behind the ball, roughly in line with the player's nose, and then moves on upward to collect the ball. With active footwork and a turn on through of the body there should be a definite sensation of rather more weight remaining on the tips of the toes of the right foot than with the other clubs.

To practise the correct contact with the driver, set up addressing an imaginary ball, having a feeling of sitting slightly towards the right foot. Concentrate on practice swings where the club very definitely brushes the ground, with a sensation of bouncing upwards a little, the contact being a good eight inches behind your imaginary ball. This should give you the feeling of the correct weight distribution. With the ball it should be much the same except that the clubhead should skim the ground rather than actually bouncing on it.

Other driving exercises

As a second exercise practise with the ball, tee it up in the correct place well forward in the feet but with your clubhead initially set opposite the middle of your stance and so several inches behind the ball. Then edge the clubhead forward to the ball, feeling that the right shoulder drops under in so doing rather than coming round. Experiment with adopting the set-up in this way and experiment also at starting with the clubhead several inches behind the ball, and even looking a little behind the ball until the more upward strike can be appreciated.

The good player who finds trouble from time to time with the driver contact, perhaps producing the odd skied shot, can usually work through the problem if it arises during play by simply teeing the ball a little lower. But to correct the fault in particularly high. This means that the ball can only be solidly hit with the player staying behind the ball correctly with a definite feeling of having to hit up on the ball. Most good golfers find that the longest and best driving occurs with a feeling of being comfortable from a ball teed high. It usually means the body is set well behind the ball at address and through impact, with more time to accelerate the clubhead into the ball.

Monitoring direction

Many players who hit the ball offline simply don't start

it out on target. There is often no real reason for this other than a poor sense of direction. To check this, preferably on a driving-range mat, position a coin or tee peg about 18 inches ahead of the ball directly on line with the target. Get someone to sit or squat behind the line of the shot to check whether the ball starts off on line.

FULLSWING EXERCISES

The inside attack

Most club golfers tend to hit the ball from out to in, i.e. with a left-aimed attack. This tends to arise from taking the club back on an outside or straight path, rather than swinging it back on the inside, and goes hand in hand with a steep backswing and attack and sliced shots. The path which the clubhead should travel back on an inside curve and attack the ball on a curve, with the ball flying off at a tangent to this curve on target. The smoother the curve as a rule the better, but never with any feeling of swinging the clubhead back on a straight line or through on a straight line. Swinging the club is much the same in principle as swinging a racket, where the racket head automatically moves round and behind the player going back and attacks the ball in a curve. To encourage this curved attack when practising on a driving range, mark the curved path with a piece of chalk, feeling that the clubhead travels back and through on it. To most club golfers it feels awkward to take the club back sufficiently on the inside. In attacking the ball on a curved path, the feeling may need to be one of hitting the ball with an exaggeratedly in-to-out attack, with the right elbow almost brushing the body before impact.

Most players who slice the ball attack it with too

steep a path, the clubhead coming slightly across the line of the shot from the outside. Low-handicap players often find it hard to believe the tendency to attack the ball from the outside and resist the idea of striking the ball in a more curved path. An exercise to encourage the correct path and to monitor precisely what happens, is to strike the ball with a light paper or plastic cup (or some similar object) positioned about 12 to 15 inches behind the ball and fractionally outside it. The best place to practise this is on a driving range when the ball can be set up uniformly on the mat. The edge of the cup nearest to you will need to be just outside the furthest side of the ball. This gives room for the toe of the club to miss it on the backswing and encourages the player to pass inside it in the attack. Clearly an out-to-in attack will smash the cup en route to the ball. Once a player can see the path of the club he can usually begin to make the correction, combining the feeling of an inside attack with a shallower one. Conversely trying for a shallower attack will often encourage a more inside one. The player who slices will usually need to work at a combination of this feeling of an inside, curved attack with a loosening of the hands and wrists and turning both hands to the right on the club to square up or slightly close the clubface through impact.

Folding the left arm

In the backswing the left arm should stay straight to produce width and consistency. But once the clubhead passes impact the left arm must start to turn and fold in precisely the same way as the right one did in the backswing. Ideally at address the left arm should hang so that the elbow bone points almost downwards towards the left hip rather than out towards the target. This is the way it is going to fold in the throughswing, folding neatly into the body and never staying stiff, and then breaking out towards the flag. Just beyond impact there is a point where both arms are flung out into an extended position. They are straight but in full shots not stiff. The left one must then start to turn and fold, elbow in, until the arm forms a nice, neat right angle at the end of the swing. There are several ways of practising this, one of which is to hold the club in the left hand grasping the inside of the elbow with the right hand. Swing the club through as though starting the throughswing, with very little backswing, and just feel the right hand pulling the left elbow in into a folding position. The left elbow should remain in front of you and visible out of the corner of the left eye. Precisely the same should happen in the swing. A left arm which stays too straight and stiff will usually result in the elbow moving out and behind you in the follow through.

Understanding footwork

In the backswing the body turns. Weight is transferred round onto the ball of the left foot and heel of the right. The left heel may rise or it may stay down. What it must *not* do is to roll onto the inside of the foot. In the downswing weight is thrust back onto the left heel so that it is firmly on the ground through impact, the right foot spinning up on the toes. Always check the balance, feeling the weight on the left heel, so that the left toes are free and relaxed.

Leg action through the ball

By the end of the swing the hips and body should be turned through to face the target. To achieve this the left heel must push firmly to the ground by impact, the right foot must spin up on the tips of the toes by the finish and the left leg must twist and straighten or virtually straighten to allow the hips through. The action of the left leg can prove difficult for many players. At address the left foot is turned out slightly, perhaps 20 degrees at the most. It stays in the same position through impact, meaning that the leg has to twist with the knee and hip facing the target. Often players have insufficient flexibility in the leg, with the result that it stays bent and leaves the hips facing right of target, usually resulting in shots pushed right or with unsuitable force from the shoulders. To practise this movement and loosen up the leg, stand with the feet apart, no club, and turn to the left, the leg twisting and straightening and the right foot spinning up on the toes. Having adopted this position, ease the hip and leg round, with a kind of bouncing action, until the movement begins to feel comfortable. The movement would of course be less important in the swing with the left foot turned out more. The danger would be that this could inhibit the backswing turn.

Grooving the finish

Many golfers spend time trying to groove a backswing without appreciating the importance of a grooved finish. The club can only be accelerated through impact providing there is space for a free followthrough. Any action where the swing beyond the ball is inhibited usually results in loss of potential clubhead speed the wrists frequently blocking the clubface open and tending to slice. Ideally at the end of a full drive the shaft of the club should settle against the player's left shoulder or back, with both arms folded and the hands somewhere beside the left ear. Frequently the problem is that the player swings the club too near his head. With an inhibited finish, saving himself from being hit on the top or back of the head. The need is to groove the finish until the club swings freely clear of the head and rests on the shoulder.

The followthrough can be practised quite simply by adopting the address position and without any backswing turning to face the target, folding the arms to let the club hang loose on the left shoulder. As a first stage turn through and take the club roughly hip height, feeling the toe of the club pointing directly upward. From there fold both arms, hand beside the left ear, club hanging loosely onto the shoulder with the elbows perhaps six inches or so apart, in approximate right angle and out in front of you. Keep repeating this movement, letting feet and legs turn through freely, until the swing is grooved and the club is always clear of the head. The feeling at the end of the swing should be of the chin being tucked in, never forced out by the right shoulder, and your view of the imaginary target would be with the right eye looking just past the right arm. Practise the throughswing until it is repetitive and then gradually add the backswing so that the two fall into place. With the ball aim for the same movements, emphasizing the feeling of the club-shaft—not the rubber grip—settling onto the left shoulder.

Practising with arms together

An excellent exercise for grooving the throughswing and for ensuring that the left elbow folds inwards instead of breaking out, is to practise with the elbows forced together. This also encourages a neat backswing position. Ideally use a piece of strong two-to three-inch elastic, sewn to form a loop or figure of eight, large enough to fit above both elbows. With the arms give in the elastic, the left arm is brought across to the right shoulder and the right elbow kept in on the backswing. In the followthrough the resistance of the elastic forces the left arm to begin to fold in instead of being allowed to break unsuitably outwards. It is perfectly possible to hit full shots up to the driver with this, and will often produce quite easily the feeling of the right movements.

The up-and-over finish

The ideal path of the clubhead attacking the ball is to strike the ball from 'inside', from there moving back inside but with a feeling of extension or swinging up the line of the shot. A common fault is to pull offline too soon after impact, with the result that with some shots the clubhead is offline by the moment of impact. To keep the club on target beyond impact you often need to allow the arms to fold so that the club swings out towards the target, up and over the left shoulder, without ever moving round and offline. The left arm needs to fold in and up rather than outwards. You should feel the body turning to face the target with the arms lifting and folding, and with the club travelling almost (though not quite) straight back behind you in the followthrough. The more the elbows feel close together and in front of the left shoulder, the better the line will be.

To practise this a good exercise is to stand two feet or so from a wall at your back. Don't do the backswing for it would be quite wrong to be able to swing back without the wall getting in the way. But do try the feeling of the through-swing, turning the body through and slowly lifting and folding the arms so that they swing up and over and remain clear of the wall. The feeling will be of a turn through of the body and lift of the arms. In the swing at full speed the same kind of effect can be felt.

As a point of interest most club golfers could wrongly swing back with a wall behind them, as a result of lifting the club too steeply, but would then find the throughswing inhibited. The top-class player by contrast swings the club much more behind him in the backswing, and would hit the wall at perhaps knee height, but would then tend to swing through and up and over rather than round in the followthrough.

Training balance

Good balance in the golf swing is essential. The general tendency is to fall forwards towards the ball by impact, instead of having weight firmly on the left heel. Any player told that his swing is too fast is usually guilty of bad balance, making the swing look fast and untidy. An excellent exercise is to practise hitting full shots, holding the balance at the end of the followthrough for a count of four seconds. Club golfers often find this virtually impossible at first, feeling that the weight is beginning to fall forward. By holding the followthrough it means that the swing can be checked. Have the feet worked through correctly? If there is any error it can be gradually corrected until it falls into place in the swing. Concentrating on balance usually means that the swing is kept smooth and unrushed. On the practice ground the aim should be to hold the finish for four seconds. By trying for the same effect on the course some sort of finish will usually be achieved, even if the player is suffering from tiredness or pressure towards the end of the round.

Kneeling to feel the plane

Many club golfers consistently swing with too steep a plane, encouraging a slice. A flatter plane encourages a draw. For the good golfer who wants to feel a flatter plane, an excellent exércise is to kneel down and hit the ball with a driver. Anything but a very flat plane tends to crash onto the ground many inches behind the ball. A flat plane can produce a shallow attack and will often give the player the feeling of a draw, which he can then transfer to his ordinary standing-up address position.

Flattening the plane

A good exercise for flattening the plane of swing, particularly for the person who slices, is to practise with the feet below the ball, perhaps a foot or so. This automatically means that the plane of swing should be more horizontal, with a shoulder turn rather than dip. Ideally this can be tried first with one of the longer clubs, perhaps a 4-iron, gradually getting the same feeling with the shorter clubs and with the ball nearer the level of the feet.

Keeping the head still

Ideally the head should stay still and the eyes look at the ball through impact. It is a common problem to find players who simply cannot keep their head still through impact. Often this is a result of holding the head too low at address. Wearers of glasses often have this problem—bifocals almost always produce quite the wrong position.

The feeling should be one of looking down the

face, not with the head over in a near horizontal position. The higher the head is held at address, the easier it is to keep the head still. For the player who lifts the head, the thought must often be of standing with 'head up' rather than keeping the head down.

But what can also cause problems is the relationship of the chin and shoulders. In the backswing the left shoulder should cover the chin and almost a little of the mouth. In the throughswing the same should happen, with the right shoulder covering the chin and part of the mouth as the arms swing through and up. Players who have difficulty in keeping their head still often let the right shoulder move under the chin in the downswing, so that the chin pokes out. The right shoulder often then gives the chin a hefty punch from beneath; forcing it up. This shows up at the end of the swing with the chin out instead of tucked in. It is a fault that is particularly likely to happen for anyone with relatively narrow shoulders and a longish neck, and is therefore one from which women are more likely to suffer than men! To correct this, practise swinging back and through, with three-quarter-length swings, covering the chin on both backswing and throughswing with the appropriate shoulder. Initially opening the mouth slightly, tongue down, can make the feeling easier, pushing the chin into the right position.

For the player whose head moves forward through impact the easiest way of checking this is to hold the followthrough, then to look back down to the original ball position to monitor any movement. Gradually it should be easier to stay in position, combining this with active legwork.

Developing clubhead speed

To produce length to a shot the clubhead needs to move at maximum speed through impact. To produce clubhead speed there needs to be a feeling of looseness and freedom in the hands and wrists. Anyone in search of more length should loosen the grip and have plenty of practice swings, feeling the hands swishing the club through, with the right arm folding in the backswing *and* the left arm folding in the throughswing. The looser this can be, the more the weight and speed of the clubhead can be felt.

An excellent exercise for developing clubhead speed is to swing the club back and through, back and through, with a continuous action for ten or twelve swings, feeling that the arms travel a comparatively short distance but that the wrists and hands produce as full a swing back and through as possible with the clubhead. Once this feeling is achieved, strengthen the hands by this same back and through swinging in some thickish rough. Emphasis should be on the hands, wrists and forearms turning and swishing, without any feeling of power or force from the shoulders.

Finding a natural swing

The good golfer can often feel he loses his natural swing, becoming uncomfortable at address or in the swing itself. A great exercise for finding the real swing and getting rid of minor problems is to line up a row of ten or twelve balls, hitting fairly quickly one after another, setting up to each, finishing each swing, but trying to minimize thinking. By the end of the row of balls, the natural swing and address position will often return.

7

DOWNSWING

Most teachers agree that the downswing starts with the movement of weight back on to the left side although many amateur golfers may not agree. Photographs show that the hips initiate the downswing as they unwind. As the hips return to square, the arms start their downward movement before the shoulders start their journey back to the square to target line. The arms can produce a great deal of clubhead speed as the right arm straightens to wards impact.

The object of the downswing is to return your body, and the club, back to the same position as before the backswing began. Try to do this in slow motion, for a while, then gradually build up the speed. This is a great way to practise the correct 'squaring up' action of the downswing.

The old 'late hit' advice, has damaged more golf swings than anything else. Late means exactly that—too late! We agree with the saying 'What is wrong with being a little early', or even better still, on time? Late hitting is caused by the body racing the arms and the club to the ball during the downswing. We prefer to hit 'on time', meaning the body and arms delivering the blow together.

Few players realize that the backswing and downswing planes are not the same. We do try to keep them the same, but because the weight changes during the backswing and downswing these swing paths differ. In general, really good players drop their arms and the club on the 'inside plane' on the way back to the ball. Poor players, and beginners in particular, do the reverse. Their plane is often quite good on the backswing but very much on the outside on the downswing. This usually is because the body races the club which, in turn, is delivered too late. As soon as the clubhead is delivered on time, the right side should move past the ball as the left side clears, allowing the club and arms to drive towards the target.

As we all know, the right arm folds and the right elbow tends to point to the ground on the backswing; but on returning to the ball, or during the downswing, the right arm must straighten. This straightening action actually helps square up the clubface, and also accelerates it. Very few golfers, even the better ones, talk about the right arm function during the swing, but this is usually the right-hander's strongest arm and must be used. Many players feel that the left arm is the key. After all, it certainly stays fairly straight on the backswing and downswing, keeping the arc constant but the weakest arm must not be the dominant one. Quite simply, the left arm guides the club by staying straight, but the right side and arm deliver the power. The modern saying amongst the world's great players is now, 'You cannot hit too early, if you shift your weight first, on the downswing.' Try it, it really does work.

The ultimate, though, for everyone is to use

everything-both feet, legs, arms and hands, all have a part to play, and it's an equal part. Do not take on passengers. They all have a job to do.

Follow-through

At impact, the club and body position should be roughly the same as it was at address. To and the follow-through, the right knee must kick in towards the left, at the same time as the left side (in particular the left hip) turns away from the target line. This turning away enables the club and arms to accelerate down the target line and on to a fairly high finish. There should be no real conscious effort to glue the head down after hitting the ball. As the club and body turn away after impact the head will follow into a position which will make watching the flight of the golf ball quite natural. An effort should be made to drive the clubhead down the line to the target after impact. This action starts the ball on the intended line and assures a good contact.

We always encourage my pupils to practise their finishing position as this is an excellent exercise for achieving good balance. A swing with good balance is a safe and consistent one. Get used to finishing in the same position with every long shot. We all practise our backswing a great deal but few players think of making a proper balanced follow-through. Make a point of practising the complete swing and learn true consistency.

8

ETIQUETTE

The rules of etiquette are not strict formalities that complicate play; rather, they simplify and enhance the game. Observance of these rules makes it possible to play better golf and to enjoy the game more, to keep the course in good condition, and to allow more people to play golf by speeding up play. Strict adherence to the rules of etiquette should be routine practice for all players.

CREATING A QUITE ATMOSPHERE

1. You and all golfers have a common purpose—to play your best game. Considerate and courteous actions set the stage for accomplishing this goal.
2. Good golf requires concentration. Remain quiet when a player is either preparing to play or is playing a shot.
3. Stand quietly and out of range of any player making a stroke. Stand out of any line of play.
4. Be careful not to disturb players outside your group. For example, the noise of loud talk carries to other parts of the course, thus distraction players in distant areas.
5. Frustrations resulting from hitting unsatisfactory

shouts or getting bad breaks are not justifications for unpleasant behaviour. Complaining, using offensive language, and club throwing are examples of unacceptable actions.

CARE OF THE GOLF COURSE

1. Replace all divots and press them firmly in place. Avoid taking divots with practice swings.
2. Walk carefully on the putting green to avoid marring the surface. Do not step or stand at the edge of the hole. On the practice putting green, stand away from any hole when playing the ball to another cup.
3. Repair ball marks on the putting green. Either with a tee or with a fork-like metal tool (available at golf shops for a nominal cost), lift up and press back the grass around the pit mark, leaving a level surface.
4. After removing the flagstick from the hole, lay it down. Do not drop or throw it on the green.
5. After putting out, lift the ball out of the hole with your hand. Do not twist the putter blade within the cup to retrieve the ball. Such a practice can mar the walls and edges of the hole.
6. Keep all carts (motorized and hand) well away from the greens and aprons and off the teeing grounds. When driving motorized carts, stay on the cart paths as much as possible. Follow the course rules.
7. When leaving a bunker, smooth out the surface so that its condition is as good or better than when you entered it.

8. Do not discard litter on the course. Do your part to maintain the beauty of the golf course.

PLAYING WITHOUT DELAY

1. Remember—you are one of many golfers paying for the privilege of playing on the course. Play without delay. Follow practices that will help speed up play.
2. If you are new to the game, be ready to play. Have a knowledge of safety, etiquette, and rules, and possess basic skills in the strokes before you attempt to play on the course.
3. You will need your own set of clubs, a golf bag, balls, and tees. During play, do not borrow clubs from another player.
4. Before starting a round, note the name and number of your golf ball. Also, follow the United States Golf Association (USGA) recommendation of placing a distinguishing mark on the ball so that it can be easily identified without picking it up. If, however, you are unable to see an identifying mark, you may mark and lift the ball, but only after announcing your intention to do so.
5. Avoid delaying play by taking numerous practice swings. If any practice swings are taken, try to limit the number to one or two.
6. Be ready to play when it is your turn. Planning ahead for some strokes is possible.
7. Any instruction should be incidental, if at all. No play should be delayed because one person is attempting to teach another.

8. After you hit a shot, watch the ball and spot its position carefully so that you can walk directly to it. Also, watch the stroke results of other players in your group so that, if necessary, you can help in any ball search.
9. When your ball is on the wrong fairway, permit players playing that hole to have the right-of-way. Avoid interfering with other players.
10. If your is delaying play by failing to keep its place on the course (falling behind the group ahead by one clear hole), either speed up your play and regain your proper position or invite the players following to play through. Likewise, if your group to play through. Wait until the players are out of range before resuming play.
11. At some golf courses on par-3 holes, golfers who have reached the putting green will invite players of the following group to hit their tee shots. While waiting for the group behind to hit their shots, the players on the green should stand off the putting surface, in back of the green, and to one side of the line from the tee to the flagstick.

ON THE PUTTING GREEN

1. Place your golf bag or cart well off and to one side or back of the putting green nearest the next tee.
2. Do not step or stand in any line of play. Check your shadow. See that it does not cast in another player's line of putt or over the hole.
3. Mark and lift your ball when requested to do so. To mark the ball position, place a small coin or marker behind the ball. If the marker is in another player's

line of putt, measure out the necessary putterhead-lengths to one side and move the marker to this spot. Follow the same procedure when replacing the ball to its original position.

In stroke play, if a ball lies close to the hole, as after a first putt, the player may putt out rather than mark the ball. This option speeds up play. But never stand in a line of play to hole out.

4. When attending the flagstick, stand to one side of the hole, at arm's length, and hold the stick and the flag (if within reach). See that your shadow does not cast in the line of play. The stick should be held in the centre of the hold until removal is necessary. After removing the flagstick, lay it down where it will not interfere with play. When all players are on the putting green or close to it, a player whose ball lies close to the hole usually offers to attend the flagstick.
5. After all players of your group have holed out, be willing to do your part in replacing the flagstick. Leaving this responsibility to the player putting out last indicates a lack of sportsmanship and may delay play.
6. After your group has holed out, replace the flagstick, leave the putting green immediately, and proceed to the next tee. Never remain on the putting green to review play of the hole or to mark scores on the score card. Do not take practice shots that will delay play.

In the bunker

1. Leave your golf bag or cart well outside the edge of the bunker.

2. Enter the bunker at the lowest bank and take the shortest route to the ball.
3. Before you walk into a bunker to play your shot, check to see whether the rake is nearby. If it is not, secure and place it near you, but where it will not interfere with play. With the rake close at hand, you can rake the sand as you walk from the trap.
4. Avoid entering or standing in a bunker when another golfer is playing from it.
5. On leaving the bunker, rake or in some manner smooth out all footprints and marks, thus leaving the surface of the sand in perfect condition.

9

RULES AND REGULATIONS

Golfers should have a thorough knowledge of the rules because only then can they play golf properly. To resolve rules, questions that may arise during play, the USGA recommends that all golfers carry rule books as part of their golfing equipment.

Types of competition

The two main types of golf competition are *stroke play* and *match play*. In stroke play, the person with the lowest score for the stipulated number of rounds, usually four rounds (72 holes), is the winner. If two or more players are tied fro first place at the end of a tournament, these players either play an 18-hole round, or they play one or more extra holes, and the first player to make the low score on a hole is the winner. In stroke competition, all players are properly referred to as *competitors*, except that, within a playing group, the contestants are called *fellow-competitors*.

Match play competition is based on the number of holes won, not the total score for a round. In a single match, a player competes against only one other player, the *opponent*. They play until one person is more holes ahead than there are holes remaining to be played in the match. If the match is tied at the end of the stipulated round, players usually continue play until one player wins a hole. Match play is an elimination-type tournament, so in the final round, only two players remain to compete for the championship.

Rules for teeing off

1. Play is started at each hole by teeing the ball within the teeing ground. This area, two club-lengths in depth, is bounded in the front and on the sides by the outer edges of the tee markers.
2. Honour, the privilege of teeing first, is usually decided by lot on the first tee. After the first hole, honour is decided by scores on the previous hole. The person with the score shoots first, and the others follow according to their scores. If two or more players score the same on a hole, they tee off in the order they followed on the previous tee.
3. The ball is in play after a stroke is made from the tee. If a player, in addressing the ball not yet in play, accidentally knocks the ball off the tee, it may be teed again without penalty.
4. If a player swings at an misses the ball on the tee, the stroke counts—the ball is in play. No ball is in play if the tee shot is lost or hit out of bounds, or, in stroke play, when the competitor plays the ball from outside the teeing ground.

General rules

1. After teeing off, the players continue to strike the ball, in turn, until they hole out. The ball should be played as it lies and not be touched except to strike it, unless situations or rules permit or require otherwise.

2. The ball farthest from the hole is played first.
3. Any attempt to hit the ball is counted as a stroke, whether or not the ball is struck.
4. When the ball is in play, the player may *not* press or stamp down ground, or break, bend, or remove anything fixed or growing. However, the surface on the teeing ground being played may be improved.
5. If, after addressing the ball in play, the ball moves, the penalty is one stroke, and the ball must be replaced.

   When a player accidentally moves a ball in searching for it in such areas as casual water, ground under repair, or a hole or runway made by a burrowing animal, the ball is replaced without penalty, unless the player elects to take relief from the situation.
6. Loose impediments, such as fallen leaves, pebbles, worms, and insects that interfere with play, may be moved. If a ball lie in a hazard, however, loose impediments may *not* be touched or moved.

   Through the green, if after moving a loose impediment within one club-length of the ball, the moves before the player has played it, the penalty is one stroke and the ball must be replaced.
7. In certain situations, a player may lift or be required to lift a ball and place or drop it.

   To drop a ball, a player stands erect, facing any direction, holds the ball at shoulder height with the arm extended, and drops the ball. The ball must be dropped in an area prescribed by the rule involved. For instance, when taking relief from a cart path, the ball is dropped within one club-length of the nearest point of relief, not nearer the hole, without penalty.

8. When a ball lies on the wrong putting green, the ball must be lifted and dropped off the putting green within one club-length of the nearest point of relief, not nearer the hole and not in a hazard, without penalty.

9. *Movable obstructions*, such as water hoses, rakes, trash containers, and benches that interfere with play, may be moved.

   If a player moves such an obstruction and the ball moves, the ball must be replaced without penalty.

10. *Immovable obstructions* include paved cart paths, shelters, and sprinkler heads.

    Through the green, if a ball lies in or on an immovable obstruction or if the obstruction interferes with the player's stance or swing, the ball may be lifted and dropped within one club-length of the nearest point of relief without penalty.

    If an immovable obstruction interferes with play in a bunker, the ball must be dropped in the bunker. If on the putting green, the already stated conditions exist, or it the obstruction is situated between the ball on the putting green and the hole, the ball may be lifted and placed at the nearest point of relief without penalty. In a water hazard, no relief is allowed without penalty.

11. Through the green, if a ball lies in casual (a temporary accumulation of water) or if the casual water interferes with the player's stance or swing,

the ball may be lighted and dropped within one club-length of the nearest point of relief, not nearer the hole, without penalty.

If a ball lies in casual water in a bunker, the ball must be dropped in the bunker, not nearer the hole, without penalty, or dropped outside the bunker with a penalty of one stroke.

If on the putting green the already stated conditions exist, or if the causal water is between the ball on the putting green and the hole, the ball may be lifted and placed, not nearer the hole, without penalty.

The rule for relief from casual water also applies to such situations as ground under repair, and a hole, runway, or cast made by a burrowing animal. Except when the ball lies in a water hazard, no relief is allowed from a hole, runway, or cast made by a burrowing animal.

Procedures for determining the nearest point of relief for immovable obstructions and from such areas as ground under repair and casual water ate the same.

12. In stroke play, the penalty for playing a wrong ball, except from a hazard, is two strokes. The player must then play the correct ball. The strokes played with the wrong ball are not counted in the score.

    In much play, the penalty for playing a wrong ball, except from a hazard, is loss of hole. Any strokes played with the wrong ball from a hazard are not counted in the player's score.

13. If another player's ball interferes with your play,

you may request that the ball the marked and lifted.

14. You may ask only your caddie, partner, or partner's caddie for advice.
15. General penalty for breaking a rule in stroke play is two strokes; in match play, loss of hole. For example: If a player stamps down the grass in back of a ball lying on the fairway, the penalty in stroke play is two strokes and loss of hole in match play.
16. The score card should be checked for local rules and interpretations that apply to the course being played.

Rules for the putting green

1. Taking a stance with either foot touching or astride the line of putt is prohibited. The line extends from the hole to a point beyond the ball. Penalty for breach of the rule is two strokes in stroke play and loss of hole in match play.
2. When playing the ball from the putting green, request that the flagstick be attended or removed from the hole. The penalty for playing a ball from the green and having it strike the flagstick is two strokes in stroke play and loss of hole in match play.
3. In stroke play, if a ball played from the putting green strikes a fellow-competitor's ball (also on the putting green), the penalty is two strokes. If the fellow-competitor's ball is moved by the impact, it must be replaced.

   In match play, there is no penalty for a player's ball played from the putting green striking the opponent's ball, also on the green. If the opponent's ball is moved by the impact, it must be replaced.

4. When the ball lies on the putting green, it may be marked, lifted, and cleaned.
5. Sand and loose soil are considered loose impediments on the putting green only. They may be picked up or brushed aside with the hand or club. If the ball is accidentally moved in removing loose impediments on the green, it is replaced without penalty.
6. When any part of the ball overhangs the hole, the player, after walking to the hole without delay, may wait ten seconds. If the ball does not fail into the hole in that time, it is considered to be at rest.

   Breach of the ten-second rule: if after the ten-second period, a ball lying two on the edge of the hole falls into the cup, the player's score for the hole is 2 plus one penalty stroke—a 3.

Rules for hazards

1. By USGA definition, hazards are bunkers and water hazards (including lateral water hazards). A bunker is usually a depressed area of bare ground covered with sand, frequently called a sand trap, but correctly referred to as a bunker. Grass-covered areas within or surrounding the bunker are not parts of the hazard.

   The limits of water hazards are usually defined by stakes or lines: yellow for water hazards and red for lateral water hazards. Marked boundaries (lines and stakes) are within the hazards. The grass-covered areas or any dry ground within the indicated margins of the water hazard are part of the hazard.

2. When the ball lies in a hazard, loose impediments may not be touched or moved.
3. Man-made objects, such as rakes, may be moved.
4. In addressing the ball in a hazard, you may *not* ground the club. The surface of the hazard cannot be touched before taking the forward swing to strike the ball.
5. Water hazard: If a ball is lost in a water hazard or declared impossible to play, the player may proceed under one of two options:
   A. Drop a ball under penalty of one stroke at the spot from which the original ball was played. If the original ball was played from the tee, the ball may be teed anywhere on the teeing ground.
   B. Drop a ball under penalty of one stroke any distance behind the hazard, keeping the point at which the ball last crossed the hazard margin between the hole and the spot on which the ball is dropped.
6. Lateral water hazard: If a ball is lost in a lateral water hazard or declared impossible to play, the player may choose one of three options to continue play:
   A. Drop a ball under penalty of one stroke at the spot from which the original ball was played. If the ball was played from the tee, the ball may be teed anywhere on the teeing ground.

B. Drop a ball under penalty of one stroke any distance behind the hazard, keeping the point at which the ball last crossed the hazard margin between the hole and the spot on which the ball is dropped.

C. Under penalty of one stroke, drop a ball within two club-lengths of where the ball last crossed the margin of the hazard or within two club-lengths of a point equidistant from the hole on the opposite margin of the hazard.

Ball out of bounds

A ball out of bounds when (1) all of it lies beyond the inside points of the out-of-bounds stakes or fence or (2) all of the ball lies on or beyond a line chalked to indicate out of bounds.

The penalty for hitting a ball out of bounds is one stroke, and the player loses the distance of the shot. The player plays again from where the original ball was played and adds one penalty stroke.

Lost ball

A player is allowed five minutes to search for a ball. After that time, the ball is considered lost.

The penalty for a ball lost outside of a water hazard is one stroke and loss of distance.

Provisional ball

When a ball is hit that may be out of bounds or lose outside of a water hazard, a provisional ball may be played. For example, suppose you hit a long drive from the tee toward an out-of- bounds fence. From the distant view, it is uncertain whether the ball is in bounds or out of bounds. After informing your playing companions of your intention, you may hit a provisional ball. If the original ball is in bounds, play it and pick up the provisional ball; if the original ball is out of bounds, play the provisional ball. Stroke and distance penalty applies.

Playing a provisional ball for one that may be out of bounds or lost (outside of a water hazard) saves the player the time and trouble of returning to the original spot of play to hit another ball. The provisional ball may be played up to the spot where the original ball may be lost or out of bounds.

Unplayable ball

A ball may be declared unplayable at any place on the course, except in a water hazard. The player is the sole judge as to when a ball is unplayable. For example, a ball is likely to be declared unplayable when it is lying against a tree, a large, embedded rock, or an out-of-bounds fence.

When the ball is declared unplayable, the player may proceed under any one of three options:

A. Play the next stroke at the spot from which the original ball was played, under penalty of one stroke (stroke and distance penalty).

B. Drop a ball within two club-lengths of the unplayable position, not nearer the hole, under penalty of one stroke.

C. Drop a ball any distance behind the unplayable position—keeping that point between the hole and the spot on which the ball is dropped, under penalty of one stroke.

HANDICAPS

A handicap is a number representing a golfer's playing ability. Most players score above par for 18-hole rounds; their course handicaps, which may range from 1 to 40 and above, indicate the approximate number of strokes they shoot over par. A player with a handicap of 0 averages neat par and is called a scratch golfer. The few players averaging near and below par have plus handicaps.

The USGA Handicap System provides a method of establishing course handicaps, thereby ensuring fair competition—on any course—among players of different abilities. A *handicap index,* based on a player's lowest ten of the last twenty scores, is calculated by a club or association. This index number can then be converted to a course handicap by using the USGA conversion tables posted at most course. Thus, golfers with handicap indexes can simply check the figures on the charts to find their course handicaps. For example, a golfer with a handicap index of 18.6 plays a more difficult course, rated 135, the handicap changes to 22.

Handicaps equalize competitive play. In an 18-hole stroke event, a net score is computed for each player by subtracting the player's handicap from the actual (gross) score.

In match play, the golfer with the higher handicap is allowed to subtract stroked from certain holes. For example, two opponents have handicaps of 7 and 4. The player with the 7-handicap subtracts one stroke from each of the scores on the holes with handicap ratings of 1, 2, and 3. On the score card, the three holes rated most difficult on the White and Blue courses are 5, 10, and 8; on the Red course, 5, 14, and 1. The player with a 4-handicap gives the opponent with a 7-handicap one stroke on each of these holes.

To maintain a correct and up-to-date handicap index, players must report all scores as per USGA regulations.

SELECTION OF ACCESSORIES AND EQUIPMENT

Comfortable and appropriate sports clothes should be worn for golf. Complete lines of attractive golf clothes for men and women are sold in many stores and course golf shops. Some golf courses have rather strict dress codes. You might want to check on such regulations before visiting a new club or course.

The preferred shoes for playing are golf shoes with spikes or with some kind of "traction" soles. They will help you to maintain your balance in swinging and also will make walking on the course easy. Low-heeled shoes must always be worn on the course. Many players wear either a glove on the left hand or gloves on both hands. Gloves may be an aid in holding the club or on provides protection from the sun.

If you plan to walk the course and carry your clubs, choose a lightweight bag with good balance. A variety of golf bags is available. Select one that best suits your needs. Hand carts are popular accessory items. Hand carts and motorized carts can be rented at most courses.

Golf balls vary in compression. For the expert, long-hitting player, a high-compression ball (rated near 100) is preferred. Average golfers find lower compression halls more suitable to their games. Balls with cut-resistant covers are favoured by many players.

Choose a putter that you like. Most golf shops will allow you to use and test putters on a practice putting green or on an indoor putting mat. A selection can be made from a wide variety of new and used putters.

In selecting irons and woods, choose clubs that fit you because, with them, you can play your best golf. Your strength, body build, and swing are some factors to consider in proper fitting. Before buying any clubs, talk with one or more golf professionals or trained salespersons and have them check your swing. They can then make a judgment as to what clubs suit you best. These services are free.

Golf shops offer players a great variety of matched sets of clubs in different styles and costs; some shops carry suitable used sets. For beginning golfers and some novices, starter sets consisting of seven or fewer clubs are adequate: A typical seven-club set includes the 3-, 5-, 7-, and 9-irons, the 1- and 3- or (4, 5)-woods, and putter. Playing with fewer clubs makes the game less complicated and does not deter progress in developing skill.

Because of the differences in height, strength, and hand size between men and women, clubs differ in club shaft flexibility, grip size, and weight. For the average man golfer, the R-shaft (regular) is the best choice; for average women golfers, the L-shaft is best. Players with above-average power and strength may choose clubs with stiffer shafts, while golfers with less-than-average strength may be helped by more flexible shafts.

Total weight and swingweight are considered in fitting clubs. Simply stated, swingweight is a measurement of the clubhead weight in proportion to the shaft and grip weight. This proportional relationship is an important factor in the "feel" and balance of the club, as is the flex of the shaft during the swing. In general, the swingweight of women's clubs ranges from C-0 to C-9; is men's clubs, swingweight is D-0 and above.

Much experimentation, testing, and research are being done to produce clubs that offer more accuracy and greater distance. New designs and new construction materials continue to be introduced into the golf club market. Your best source of information on current developments in club technology is your golf professional.

INDEX